religion and life of Israel. It is not an exaggeration to say that some knowledge of Babylonian religion is indispensable for a proper understanding of the development of Hebrew religion. Hence this book will be of service to students of the Old Testament as well as to those who are interested in the comparative study of religion.

This is the American edition of a work which is also published in Great Britain.

THE AUTHOR

S. H. HOOKE, who holds degrees from the universities of Oxford and London, is a renowned authority on Biblical archaeology. He was formerly Davidson Professor of Old Testament Studies at the University of London, and is now professor emeritus. He has published many distinguished volumes on Semitic and comparative religions.

BABYLONIAN AND ASSYRIAN RELIGION

BABYLONIAN AND ASSYRIAN RELIGION

S. H. HOOKE

UNIVERSITY OF OKLAHOMA PRESS • NORMAN

Assyro-Babylonian religion

BY THE SAME AUTHOR

New Year's Day. London, G. Howe Ltd., 1927.

Myth and Ritual. London, Oxford University Press, 1933.

The Labyrinth. London, Society for Promoting Christian Knowledge; New York, The Macmillan Co., 1935.

Prophets and Priests. London, T. Murby & Co., 1938.

The Origins of Early Semitic Ritual.
London, Oxford University Press, 1938.

What is the Bible? London, SCM Press, 1948.

In the Beginning. Oxford, Clarendon Press, 1948.

The Kingdom of God in the Experience of Jesus.
London, Gerald Duckworth & Co., 1949.

Alpha and Omega. Melwyn, Herts., 1961.

Babylonian and Assyrian Religion.
Norman, University of Oklahoma Press, 1963.

LIBRARY OF CONGRESS CATALOG CARD NUMBER: 63–9953

U. S. edition, 1963, from the English edition of Basil Blackwell, Oxford, 1962. Composed and printed at Norman, Oklahoma, U.S.A., by the University of Oklahoma Press. First edition.

PREFACE

APART from its own intrinsic interest, the study of the religion of the Babylonians and Assyrians has an added importance because of the great influence which the civilization and religion of those dwellers in the Tigris-Euphrates Valley had on the religion and life of Israel. It is not an exaggeration to say that some knowledge of Babylonian religion is indispensable for a proper understanding of the development of Hebrew religion. Hence this book is intended to be of service to students of the Old Testament, as well as to those who are interested in the comparative study of religions.

The bibliography at the end of this book will show the extent of my indebtedness to the labors of other scholars; but I may be allowed to add that I have read a large part of the religious texts, with the exception of those in Sumerian, in the original cuneiform texts, and I owe whatever knowledge I possess of this branch of Semitic studies to the great learning and patience of Professor Sidney Smith. My debt to him I have acknowledged in the dedication of my Schweich Lectures on *The Origins of Early Semitic Ritual.* I am also indebted to Mr. C. J. Gadd, the Keeper of the Egyptian and Assyrian Antiquities at the British Museum for much kindly help during many years. I have also found great stimulus and illumination from Professor H. Frankfort's recent books, especially from the symposium brought out under his editorship, entitled *The Intellectual Adventure of Ancient Man,* and from his recent books *Kingship and the Gods,* and *The Birth of Civilization in the Near East.* One more source of immensely important fresh knowledge must be mentioned, namely, Professor Kramer's *Sumerian Mythology.* I have also to acknowledge my debt to my wife for her great help in correcting the proofs and for many valuable suggestions.

I am very conscious of the limitations and imperfections of this book, but I hope it may be of some use to students as an introductory manual, and that it will not be too severely judged by the experts in this field of studies.

S. H. HOOKE

CONTENTS

ILLUSTRATIONS

INTRODUCTION

IT is hard to realize that very little more than a century ago the script and languages in which the records of the great civilizations of the Tigris-Euphrates Valley lay concealed were completely unknown. The recent work of Professor Mallowan on the site of Nineveh is a continuation of the work begun by Layard on that site in 1845. The immediate result of the latter's excavations was the discovery of the library of Ashurbanipal; by this spectacular discovery thousands of cuneiform tablets became available for study, and awaited the finding of the key which should unlock their secrets. This was provided by the skill and enterprise of Sir Henry Rawlinson who succeeded in deciphering the great trilingual inscription of Darius the Great on the rock of Behistun. With the key in their hands, scholars began to apply it to the decipherment of the tablets found at Nineveh, and the first sensational achievement was the work of a self-taught genius, George Smith, an assistant at the British Museum. While working at the repair of damaged tablets, he recognized one as containing the Babylonian story of the Flood, a myth which, as we shall see later, was the eleventh tablet in the famous Akkadian epic of Gilgamesh. He translated it and made public his discovery whose genuineness, in spite of much learned skepticism, was quickly vindicated.

So began the fascinating process of bringing to light after so many centuries of oblivion, the vast treasures of Sumerian, Babylonian, and Assyrian civilization. Much has been done since George Smith translated the story of the Flood and revealed to the world the astonishing resemblances between the Hebrew story of the Flood and its far more ancient Babylonian predecessor, but much remains to be done. Thousands of tablets still await transcription and translation, and all the time fresh stores of tablets from other Mesopotamian sites are constantly coming to light. Hence any book on the subject of Babylonian and Assyrian religion is bound to get out of date in a few years, as new material accumulates and is made available to students. Even the recognition of important differences between the kindred cultures of Babylon and Assyria is of comparatively recent date, and a considerable amount of obstinate skepticism had to be overcome before it was admitted that behind the civilization of Babylon and Assyria lay an older stratum, the civilization of the Sumerians, a people alien in speech and race from the Semitic invaders who conquered them and absorbed their religion and culture to a great extent, while retaining their own language, and no doubt much of their own religion and traditions.

One of the most remarkable scientific achievements of the century which has elapsed since Layard began to dig in the mounds of Kouyundjik, has been the rediscovery of so many ancient civilizations which had been partially or wholly buried beneath the soil for thousands of years. Almost within the span of a single lifetime we have seen the resurrection of Troy, of the brilliant Minoan Empire, of predynastic Egypt, of the Sumerian culture and the Babylonian and Assyrian civilizations which sprang from it, of the great Hittite Empire and the decipherment of its mysterious pictographic script, and, most recent of all, of the ancient Indian civilization at the mouth of the Indus, at Mohenjodaro and Harappa. The result has been the creation of a new general interest in how these ancient peoples lived, what they thought, and especially what kind of religion they practiced. The underlying unity of all civilization is becoming increasingly realized. Students of anthropology, the science of man, are beginning to recognize that a Babylonian myth may be as worthy of study as an Ibo myth for the light it may throw on man's early reactions to his environment, and his early social patterns. Many of the earlier textbooks on this subject have been made out of date by the rapid advance of modern knowledge. An interesting example of this is to be found in that still very valuable book, W. Robertson Smith's *Religion of the Semites*. On p. 19 of that book the statement occurs, "strictly speaking, mythology was no essential part of ancient religion." One of the most striking results of modern research into the records of early Sumerian and Babylonian religion has been the light which it has thrown on the central importance of myth in the religion of these ancient dwellers in Mesopotamia, as Robertson Smith would have been the first to acknowledge had he been living today.

Much of the new material, still rapidly increasing, is buried in the pages of encyclopedias and learned journals, and is not easily available to the ordinary reader; it is the purpose of this book to put at the disposal of such a reader the results of the most recent researches of scholars, and to give him a reliable and up-to-date account of the religious beliefs and practices of these ancient inhabitants of the Tigris-Euphrates Valley, whose civilization has exercised so great an influence upon the other peoples of the Near East, and not least upon the Hebrews.

It has been pointed out above that scholars now recognize the existence of important differences between the civilization of Assyria and that of Babylon, in spite of the facts, (*a*) that an earlier Sumerian culture underlay the civilization of both countries; (*b*) that both Assyrians and Babylonians were of Semitic stock and spoke very closely related forms of Semitic language; (*c*) that the Assyrians borrowed largely from the Babylonians especially in the sphere of law and religion. Hence, in this book the general outline of the religion of the Babylonians and Assyrians is mainly concerned with the elements common to both countries, but such outstanding differences as occur will be pointed out in their place. In this connection it may be relevant to quote the judgment of Professor Sidney Smith, the leading modern authority on the history of Assyria: "The lack of individuality then in the Assyrians was no more remarkable than that of the Romans who similarly accepted a religion not their own. It is more profitable to turn to the very few distinctive features of their religious practice, and only two seem to be established for the period under consideration (i.e., middle of the second millennium B.C.). One consists in the position of the national god, Ashur. . . . The other lies in the prominence of the gods of war, or of the warlike characteristics of well-known gods. . . . It is extremely difficult on the evidence now available to form a just estimate of Assyrian religion, and of the particular activities it called forth; but the expressions of many modern writers, which would lead to the opinion that that land has nothing of interest to reveal to the student of human development, are very wide of the mark. The taste of the Assyrians was, moreover, catholic. They were not bound to observe any of the broad differences that were recognized in Babylonia. The Gilgamesh epic, of which the only Babylonian edition, which dates from about 2100–1900 B.C., was found at Erech, was never mentioned apparently by the priests of Babylon: the Assyrians studied it. The strange poem, 'Let me praise the lord of wisdom,' which propounds the same problem as the book of Job, though it states the matter in a different way, was acceptable to them. To this catholicity no small debt was owed by the ancient world; and to it we owe our knowledge of these works, which deserve a more searching analysis than they have yet received for their importance in the history of the development of the human spirit to be appreciated. If a broad taste for the best available is a mark of culture, then the Assyrians were a cultured people; their crass superstitions, their readiness to adopt religious and semireligious beliefs, and their devotion to the collection of all religious literature must not be allowed to obscure their merit."[1]

This brief summary of the relation between Assyrian and Babylonian religion is given here in the introduction to this book to explain why it is not possible to present Assyrian religion in a separate treatment. Broadly speaking, Babylonian religion, built

[1] *Early History of Assyria*, 340–41.

on the foundation laid by the Sumerians, was a magico-religious system based on the fear of evil spirits, and other incalculable elements in the social environment. It could not be taken piece-meal, but had to be adopted as a whole by the Assyrians, with such minor variations as have been mentioned above.

BABYLONIAN AND ASSYRIAN RELIGION

CHAPTER I

SOURCES OF OUR KNOWLEDGE

UNTIL the labors of archeologists in recent times had brought to light the great stores of cuneiform tablets buried in the ruins of ancient Mesopotamian cities, our knowledge of early Babylonian and Assyrian religion was mainly derived from early Greek antiquarians, such as Berosus and Herodotus, and from the Old Testament, and was necessarily scanty and one-sided. But today the situation has been completely transformed. From the great library of Ashurbanipal at Nineveh, from Erech, Ur, Kish, and many other ancient cities of Mesopotamia, vast numbers of clay tablets, inscribed in the cuneiform script which the valley dwellers invented, have been unearthed, transcribed, and translated. A very large number of these tablets contain religious material of the greatest interest, ranging in time from the earliest stages of Sumerian religion, down to the Seleucid epoch. The various types of religious literature are enumerated and described below, but before we deal with them we must first take a glance at the other sources from which our knowledge of Babylonian and Assyrian religion is derived.

Among the objects discovered in the course of excavation have been great quantities of cylinder seals, both large and small. These are made of some hard stone, such as steatite or haematite, and are generally engraved with the name of the owner and a representation of a god engaged in some ritual act. These seals have been a most valuable source of knowledge concerning Babylonian gods and ritual scenes during different periods of religious development. Moreover, the excavation of the temples has shown the plan and disposition of the various buildings and their uses, and has also yielded many cult-objects giving further light on temple ritual. Another important source of knowledge has been the inscriptions on steles and statues, such as the preface to the famous Code of Hammurabi, engraved on a pillar of black basalt, and giving information about the religious functions of the king.

Returning now to the various types of religious literature represented in the tablets, we have the following:

a) *Myths.* We shall have more to say later about the relation of myth and ritual in Babylonian religion, but while some of the Babylonian myths have come down to us in connection with a ritual, others have survived in an independent literary form. There is the myth of Creation which exists in several forms: the best known is what is called the Epic of Creation, recited at the great New Year Festival; there is the popular myth of the semidivine hero Gilgamesh, whose adventures have been preserved in several recensions; embedded in the Gilgamesh Epic is the best-known version of the Babylonian myth of the Flood with which the Hebrew stories of the Flood are closely connected. Other well-known myths are the myth of Adapa, of Etana and the Eagle, and of the descent of Ishtar into hell. These are but a few of the best-known examples of what constitutes the great body of Babylonian mythology.

b) *Liturgies.* We have a number of the prayers, hymns, and chants, which were sung by the priests at the various festivals and sacred occasions of the religious year. The most important of these is the New Year liturgy, giving us the order of worship for most of the eleven days of the feast.

c) *Ritual Texts.* We have a large number of texts giving instructions for the ritual acts of the priests on various sacred occasions, such as the dedication of a temple, the consecration of a sacred drum, the ritual for an eclipse, and many others.

d) *Incantations and Spells.* Several important collections of magical texts have been preserved, such as the collections called *Maqlu* and *Shurpu*. These consist of spells intended to protect an individual from the attacks of hostile demons and the machinations of wizards and witches.

e) *Omen Texts*. One of the functions of the Babylonian priests was the interpretation of omens. Unusual occurrences in the natural world were regarded as indicating either good or bad fortune for the individual or the community, and were recorded by the priests together with the interpretation. A large number of tablets containing collections of omens have been discovered in the excavation of various temples.

f) *Astrological Texts*. Throughout the entire history of Babylonian religion, observation of the heavenly bodies played a great part in religious belief and practice. It was thought that the movements of the stars and planets influenced the fortunes of nations and individuals, and many tablets have been discovered containing such astrological material.

This will give some idea of the varied contents of the religious literature of the Babylonians. In addition to this body of directly religious texts, there are also secular sources which give indirect information about the religion of the Babylonians and Assyrians. There is, for example, the important collection of the State correspondence of the Assyrian kings, giving much valuable information about the king's functions in state rituals, and other public aspects of the religion. Then the vast body of business documents, contracts, wills, transfers of slaves and landed property, has much to contribute to the knowledge of the religious side of social life, since hardly any kind of business transaction could take place without some kind of religious observance connected with it. Also the various collections of laws throw much light on religious beliefs and practices.

Such are the sources upon which we are now able to draw

for our knowledge of the intricate pattern of religious life among the Babylonians and Assyrians, and every year brings some fresh accession to the store.

CHAPTER II

CULTURAL BACKGROUND OF THE RELIGION

IN order to understand the nature and development of the religion of a people, it is necessary to know something of its origin and cultural background. When the ancestors of the Babylonians entered the Tigris-Euphrates Delta, they found an advanced civilization already established there. This was the work of a people to whom reference has previously been made, the Sumerians. The Babylonians and Assyrians, who were closely related in speech and in many other respects, belonged to the Semitic branch of Near Eastern peoples, but the Sumerians did not. They spoke a non-Semitic language, and their general physical characteristics were quite unlike those of the newcomers who gradually subjugated them and absorbed their culture. The Sumerians came into the delta from the mountainous country to the northeast, though it is not certain where their original home was. Their religious literature shows that they came from a region where forest trees, such as the fir and the pine, grew, which were not to be found in the low, marshy lands of the delta. During the period of Sumerian ascendancy that part of Mesopotamia which was the seat of Sumerian civilization was known as Sumer and Akkad; Sumer was the name given to the southern part of the country round the delta, while the northern portion, in which Babylon was situated, was called Akkad; hence the language spoken by the Babylonians is commonly known as Akkadian.

In this land of Sumer and Akkad the Sumerians had built up an elaborate and advanced culture whose basis was agriculture, a fact which determined the character of the religion, and upon this foundation the structure of Sumerian society rested. The unit of Sumerian political organization was the city-state, ruled over by a priest-king who bore the title of *ishshaku*, the Semitic form of the older Sumerian *patesi*. In contemporary documents he is described as "the tenant farmer of the god." He was supposed to hold the lease of his land direct from the principal god of his city, and his tenure was supposed to be renewed yearly at the New Year festival. As the representative of the god he was the head of a body of officials which controlled every aspect of communal life, and it has been said that "he united in his person the prestige attaching to 'god's tenant' with an undivided power as supreme lawgiver, judge, and commander." According to Sumerian ideas as represented in the early king-lists, kingship "came down from heaven," perhaps an intentionally vague expression suggesting that the origin of kingship lay far back in the mists of antiquity.

It has been recently suggested[1] that the earliest form of government in Mesopotamia was what is described as a "Primitive Democracy," i.e., government by the assembly of the free men of the city; actual power was in the hands of a body of elders who dealt with the day to day needs of the community, but in times of crisis chose a single individual to take control for a limited period, just as the Romans in early Republican times chose a dictator to deal with the threat of invasion, but expected him to return to the status of a simple citizen after the crisis was over. This view is perhaps supported by the fact that the Sumerian word for such an individual was *lugal*, which means "great man"; the cuneiform sign for the Sumerian word *lugal* and its Akkadian equivalent *sharru*, was the sign for "man" with the addition of something on his head, possibly a crown, which made him "great man." In the Epic of Creation, when the gods are threatened by the revolt of the underworld powers raised by Tiamat, they choose one of the younger gods, Marduk, to deal with the situation, and confer absolute power upon him. Here the myth may contain the reflection of the process of choosing the king. On the other hand, the very ancient Epic of Gilgamesh describes the hero of that story as being king of

[1] *The Intellectual Adventure of Ancient Man*, ed. H. Frankfort.

Erech, and as exercising despotic and even tyrannical power over his city. Yet even here, when war threatens the city, Gilgamesh is represented as consulting the assembly and the elders. It is possible that, as Professor Frankfort states, the source of the king's authority was his election by the assembly; yet, by the beginning of the second millennium B.C. we find Hammurabi declaring that he was "called" to the kingship by Anu and Bel, and in general the Assyrian kings in their titularies and inscriptions describe themselves as "dear to Ninib" or some other god, and represent themselves as chosen by the gods for kingship. It is therefore possible to interpret the ancient formula that "kingship came down from heaven" as implying an early belief that kingship was the gift of the gods.

A further point of importance is the existence in the early Sumerian city-state of other holders of power besides the *lugal* or king; these were the high priest, whose Sumerian title was *sangu mah*, and the city governor, or *ensi*. If the king was the god's tenant-in-chief, the high priest was the administrator of the temple revenues and leader of the community worship. He supervised the fixing of the boundaries of lands and fields leased to individuals, and placed the boundaries under the protection of the gods by the erection of boundary stones inscribed with the symbols of the gods. Professor Frankfort's description of the early organization is worth quoting here: "The land owned by the community (in the guise of the god) was divided into three parts. Some of it, *kur* land, was parceled out to provide sustenance for the members of the community who cultivated it. The sizes of those allotments differed considerably, but even the smallest contained almost an acre—enough to keep a man, and possibly a small family. Another part of the land—in one case, for instance, one fourth of the total—was reserved for the god. This was called *nigenna* land, and its produce was stored in the temple. All members of the community, irrespective of their rank or function, were obliged to cultivate this land and to undertake *corvée* on the dikes and canals insuring its irrigation.

The implements and teams of oxen and asses used for these communal tasks were kept in the stables and storehouses of the temple; they were evidently owned by the community as a whole. Grain for sowing was also supplied by the temple. Not only the produce of the fields, but implements, ritual equipment, and animals needed for sacrifice or rations for the people were likewise temple property. Furthermore, members of the community acknowledged the obligation to exercise their special skills in the service of the god. Metalworkers, stonecutters and carpenters, boatmen and fishermen, gardeners and shepherds, all worked for a certain time, or produced a certain amount of work, for the temple. Those who had special skills exercised them not only for the community but also for private trade and barter. Thus individual enterprise found a certain scope. In fact, a third type of temple land (*urula* land), was rented out for cultivation by individuals." (Frankfort, *Kingship and the Gods*, p. 221.)

The other official person, the governor or *ensi*, held a permanent position in the city, and we find the chief priest of the god who owned the city designated as *ensi* and acting as governor of the city. Hence, in the early period of political development there were three official persons upon whom the control of the city state might devolve, and, as Professor Frankfort remarks, "By Early Dynastic times one or other of these functionaries had established himself as ruler in each of the Mesopotamian cities." (Frankfort, *op. cit.*, p. 223.)

From time to time during the early dynastic period one or other of these city-states gained the leadership of the country, and gave the name to one of the various dynasties which compose the early king-lists; thus we find Kish, Erech, Ur, Isin, and Larsa, assuming the leadership at various periods, and the dynasties to which they gave their names lasted, some for a very short time, and others for 200 years or more.

But the general pattern of culture did not change with the changing dynasties; while each city had its own guardian deity,

Shamash at Sippar, Sin at Ur, Marduk at Babylon, the general plan of temple buildings, the organization of the priesthood, and the structure of society were practically the same throughout the whole of Sumer and Akkad. Concerning the temple buildings and the priesthood more will be said in a later chapter, but a few words must be said here about the social structure of the Sumerians.

The community was divided into three classes. First came the *amēlu*, or aristocracy, composed of the king, the nobles, the priesthood, government officials, and the regular soldiers. The second class consisted of merchants, farmers, artisans, and other freemen of various occupations; these were known as *mushkēnu*. The third class, upon which the structure of society rested, as it did later in Greece and Rome, consisted of slaves, either those who had been captured in war, or those who had been purchased or become enslaved through debt or other causes. These classes were far from equal before the law, and the incidence of punishment differed considerably as between the classes. It is probable that these class distinctions were of military origin.

In war the Sumerians were highly efficient, both as regards weapons and tactics; they invented the phalanx formation, afterwards exploited with such deadly effect by the Macedonians. In arts and crafts the Sumerians had reached a very high level of excellence; the technique of their goldsmiths and jewelers was hardly surpassed even by the best Egyptian craftsmen. Sumerian priests invented and developed the system of writing on clay tablets which is known as cuneiform, and which was adopted, not only by the Babylonians and Assyrians, but by the Hittites, and later by the Persians. This system was not alphabetic but syllabic and ideographic: that is, the signs of which the script was composed represented both ideas and syllables, but not letters or single sounds. Since the system was invented to express Sumerian, which was a non-Semitic language, complications ensued when it was adopted by the Babylonians to express their own speech which was Semitic. The Babylonians gave new values to the signs in the process of adapting the system to their own language; consequently a single sign might possess as many as five or six different values, making the problem of decipherment very difficult. Moreover, since the Babylonians took over from the Sumerians their pantheon and their whole religious organization with its liturgies and incantations, the Sumerian language continued to be used for religious purposes down to the Seleucid period, just as Latin continued to be the language of the Church and the law courts during the Middle Ages. Many tablets have come down to us which contain sign-lists giving in parallel columns the Sumerian and the Babylonian values of the cuneiform signs, showing that Babylonian scribes needed the help of lexicons in their use of the ancient Sumerian texts.

The Babylonians and the Assyrians brought their own gods with them when they migrated into Mesopotamia, and these gods naturally possessed Semitic names. In the process of absorbing the Sumerian culture, the invaders retained the Sumerian names of many of the gods, temple names, official titles, and names of cult-objects, while they changed some of the names and titles into Semitic forms; for example, the Sumerian name for the sun-god, Babbar, became the Semitic Shamash; the Semitic word for "temple," *hekal*, is a corruption of the Sumerian E. GAL, which means "the great house."

The famous collection of Babylonian laws made by Hammurabi is based upon earlier collections of Sumerian laws, and, indeed, almost every aspect of Babylonian and Assyrian culture has been shaped and influenced by Sumerian culture to such an extent that it is difficult to determine what elements in the religion of the Babylonians are of purely Semitic origin.

There is another aspect of the background of Babylonian religion which calls for remark, and that is the influence of the natural environment and conditions upon the religion. In both Egypt and Mesopotamia the pattern of civilization was mainly determined by the fact that rivers, the Nile for Egypt, and the Tigris and Euphrates for Mesopotamia, were the source of the life of these countries. In Egypt the Nile, worshiped as a god, was never thought of as a hostile, destructive force. Its quiet, regular flooding, controlled and distributed by a central authority, which was the cause of the early unification of Egypt under a single political monarchy, gave an element of stability to the religious pattern of Egypt which is wanting in Mesopotamia. In the latter country the creation of an ordered civilization was the result of a hard struggle against the destructive and incalculable floods to which the river valley was exposed. Hence the origin myths of Babylonia were couched in terms of a conflict with hostile powers personified as the Tiamat dragon or the Labbu monster. Egypt, on the other hand, had no Flood myth. For the same reason there was no early and stable unification of the country under a single authority, as was the case in Egypt.

A quotation from Professor Jacobsen's interesting contribution to a recent book, *The Intellectual Adventure of Ancient Man*, brings out admirably this aspect of the cultural background of Babylonian religion: "This same approach underlies the battle drama. Each new year, when floods threatened to bring back the primeval watery chaos, it was of the essence that the gods should fight again that primeval battle in which the world was first won. And so man took on the identity of a god: in the cult rite the king became Enlil, or Marduk or Assur, and as the god he fought the powers of chaos. To the very end of Mesopotamian civilization, a few centuries before our era, the king, every new year in Babylon, took on the identity of Marduk, and vanquished Kingu, leader of Tiamat's host, by burning a lamb in which that deity was incarnate." Professor Jacobsen continues, "In these festivals, which were state festivals, the human state contributed to the control of nature, to the upholding of the orderly cosmos. In the rites man secured the revival of nature in spring, won the cosmic battle against chaos, and created the orderly world each year anew out of chaos."[2]

[2] *Intellectual Adventure of Ancient Man*, 199f.

13

CHAPTER III

THE PANTHEON

ONE of the most striking features of Mesopotamian religion is the enormous number of gods whose names have been preserved in the various religious texts which have come down to us. In Tallqvist's standard book, *Akkadische Götterepitheta* (1938), the descriptive list of Akkadian gods occupies over 240 pages, and many of the names, as that scholar has said, defy all attempts to recover their meanings. Hence it is not possible here to do more than give the names and describe the functions of the most important gods of the Babylonian and Assyrian pantheon.

As far back as archeological evidence will take us the religion of the dwellers in Mesopotamia appears in an advanced stage of development, and it is impossible to give any reliable account of its origin. There is nothing, for example, in Mesopotamia corresponding to what appears to be the totemistic stage of religion in ancient Egypt. Some of the Babylonian myths show traces of a struggle between the older gods and those who attained supremacy in the pantheon at a later stage, much as we have in Greece the myth of the overthrow of Cronos by Zeus. Such myths may represent the process by which the gods of an invading people reduced to a subordinate position the gods of the earlier inhabitants of the country. It often appears, too, that in the course of such changes the dispossessed and dethroned gods became devils and evil spirits, and it is possible that this may have happened in Mesopotamia where, as we shall see later, evil spirits played an important part in the religion of Babylonia and Assyria. Moreover, Babylonian preoccupation with the spirits of the dead and their power to harm the living may well point to an animistic stage of religious development of which other traces may be seen in the use of amulets or clay figurines to protect houses or individuals.

One characteristic of Mesopotamian religion which is also to be found in other ancient religions, is to be noted, namely, its intense conservatism. For example, we find that liturgical forms and prayers which were in use in Ur and Isin about 2300 B.C. continued to be used as late as the Seleucid period, even though political changes in the interval had replaced by other gods those to whom the prayers were originally addressed.

Already in early Sumerian times, long before the rise of the first Babylonian dynasty, various lists of gods existed, and about the middle of the third millennium B.C., possibly in Erech, a standard list was drawn up. Upon this, although in course of time changes in the relative importance of various gods took place, the general order of the Babylonian and Assyrian pantheon rested.

First in this established order appears the high god, Anu, whose name in Sumerian means "heaven," and who may be said to correspond to the Greek sky-god, Zeus. In the early Sumerian period the position of Anu is relatively obscure, and his name does not occur in any of the eighteen lists belonging to this period; but from the time of Gudea, the famous priest-king of Lagash (*circa* 2060–42 B.C. according to Forrer's recent chronology), Anu begins to assume the supremacy which he retains during the subsequent history of the Babylonian religion. According to the Babylonian Epic of Creation, in the form in which it has reached us, the genealogy of Anu is traced from Apsu, the underworld ocean, and Tiamat, primeval Chaos. His abode was in the third heaven, and he was styled "Father" and "King of the Gods." No pictorial representations of Anu have come down to us, but his symbol, the sacred shrine surmounted by the divine horned cap, is often found on Babylonian boundary stones. His sacred number was 60, and the heavenly equator was the special part of the heavens assigned to him. In the early period Anu had a consort named Antu, a colourless entity without importance in the cult or mythology, but in the historical period her place as the consort of Anu was filled by Innina or

Ishtar, the great goddess, who under various names and divers forms, was the most important object of worship in the ancient Near East. It was believed that from the union of Anu and Antu, whose Sumerian name means "the earth," were born the underworld gods called the Anunnaki, and the seven evil *utukki* or demons. The most important centres of Anu's cult were Der, specially designated as Anu's city, Ur, Erech, Nippur, Lagash, where Gudea built a temple for Anu, and Sippar; in Babylon he shared a temple with Ninni and Nanai, while in Ashur there was a great double ziqqurat for Anu and Adad. In Thureau-Dangin's *Rituels Accadiens* we have the list of daily offerings for Anu's temple in Erech, the ritual for the New Year Festival of Anu in the spring and autumn, and the ritual for the making of Anu's sacred *lilissu*-drum. Anu's sacred animal was the heavenly Bull. In spite of his pre-eminence, Anu was not regarded as friendly to mankind, but was thought of rather as the god of kings and princes who were accustomed to style themselves in inscriptions as "beloved of Anu."

The second member of the great Babylonian triad of deities was Enlil or Ellil, whose name in Sumerian means "wind- or storm-god." He was specially associated with the city of Nippur, and was, like Anu, a Sumerian god who was adopted by the invading Semites. In the earlier period before Hammurabi, Enlil seems to have taken precedence over the other two gods of the triad, but from the beginning of the second millennium onwards his place is always the second. In the fragments of the older myths which lie behind the Epic of Creation in its present form, Anu seems to have suffered some disaster, and Enlil played the role of the slayer of Enmesharra and the avenger of his father Anu, a role which was later assumed by Marduk. In Sumerian and Babylonian mythology Enlil presents an ambivalent aspect. On the one hand he is bitterly hostile to mankind; it is he who is mainly instrumental in bringing about the Flood, and who is represented as being enraged at the escape of one member of the human race from destruction: on the other hand he is the creator of mankind in many of the earlier forms of the Creation myth, and a number of personal names compounded with the name of Enlil, e.g., Enlilnirari, "Enlil is my helper," show that Enlil was regarded as a source of favor and help.

One of Enlil's most important functions was the guardianship of the "tablets of destiny," the possession of which gave him power over the "destiny" of all things; in early Babylonian thought, to "fix the destiny" of anything, animate or inanimate, signified the determining of its place in the created order; in the early Hebrew form of the Creation story Adam, by giving names to the animals fixes their "destiny," that is, he assigns to them their place in the order of creation. One of the early colorful myths of the Sumerian period was the story of how the storm-bird Zu stole the tablets of destiny from Enlil, and how Enlil recovered them. A scene frequently depicted on early cylinder seals is the bringing of the captive Zu-bird, represented as half man, half bird, before Enlil for judgment.

Like Anu, Enlil is represented as having a long genealogy, and a consort, Ninlil; his chief minister was Nusku, the fire-god, and in addition he possessed the usual retinue of lesser gods who served as doorkeepers, cooks, shepherds, and messengers. The chief centre of Enlil's cult was the famous temple in Nippur, called Ekur, "The House of the Mountain," a name which passed into general use as a designation for a temple. But Enlil was worshipped in many other cities as well; he had guest rights in Gudea's Anu-temple in Lagash; an early temple in Ashur, called Eamkurkurra, "the House of the Wild Bull of the Lands," was probably an Enlil temple, and there is evidence for his worship at Borsippa.

His sacred number was 50, and the "way of Enlil," i.e., the part of the starry heavens assigned to him, lay to the north of the "way of Anu" which covered the heavenly equator. Theoretically all the stars lying more than 12 degrees north of the equator were his, and are referred to as "the stars of Enlil" in a text from Boghazköi; his special astrological symbol was the stargroup of the Pleiades, often represented on boundary stones as seven small circles.

The third and most interesting of the first triad of great gods was Enki, or, as he was generally called in the later texts, Ea. As Anu was the god of heaven, Enlil the god of the lands, i.e., of the earth, so Enki came to be regarded as specially the god of the waters, and was thought of as having his abode in the *apsu*, or abyss of waters, the underworld ocean upon which, according to Babylonian cosmology, the world rested. A favorite designation of Enki, or Ea, was *bel nimēqi* or "lord of wisdom," since he was regarded as the source of all secret magical knowledge, and also as the instructor of mankind in all the arts and crafts necessary for human well-being. It was he who had revealed to men the mysteries of writing, building, and agriculture. Water, often referred to as "water of life," was an essential element in incantations, delivering men from disease and the assaults of demons; hence Ea was, as god of the waters, specially invoked in spells and incantations, and was known as *bel shipti*, "lord of incantations."

In contrast to Anu and Enlil, both, as we have seen, regarded as hostile to mankind, Ea was thought of as specially favorable to men; in several early forms of the Creation myth he plays a part in the creation of man, and in the Flood myth it is through the intervention of Ea that Enlil's design to destroy mankind is revealed to Ut-napishtim, who thereupon builds a great boat and escapes the Flood. (See p. 66f.)

The chief centre of Ea's cult was in Eridu, at the head of the Persian Gulf, the oldest of the Sumerian cities, where he dwelt in his temple, Eengurra, and where stood his sacred *kishkanu-* tree, itself a special object of veneration. Ea's attendant was Mummu, the craftsman-god, the personification of technical skill; his consort was the goddess Damkina, and his son was Marduk, whose name is Semitic, unlike most of the older gods in the pantheon, whose names are Sumerian. With the rise of Babylon to supremacy in Mesopotamia, and possibly as the result of it,

Marduk replaces some of the older gods in the great rituals and becomes the central figure in the Babylonian cult. In Assyria, however, his place is taken by Ashur, the chief god of Assyria.

In the magical texts Ea and Marduk are usually represented as co-operating in the efficacious working of the spell or incantation, so much so that in many incantations we find the myth of Marduk consulting his father used as a regular formula; Ea answers Marduk with the words, "O my son, what dost thou not know, what more can I give thee? O Marduk, what dost thou not know, what can I add to thy knowledge? What I know, thou knowest also."

Ea's sacred number was 40, and the "way of Ea" was that part of the heavens lying 12 degrees south of the heavenly equator. Various stars and constellations are assigned to Ea in the astrological texts, and of these the two most frequently mentioned are Pisces and Aquarius. Ea's symbol, as represented on boundary stones, was either a ram's head, or the goat-fish, a mythical creature with the body of a fish and the head of a goat.

In the early lists the figure of the mother-goddess, known under various names as Ninmah, Nintu, Ninhursagga, and Aruru, was associated with the first great triad of gods. Her special function was concerned with childbirth, and as Aruru she was associated with Enlil or Ea in the creation of mankind.

Next in order in the early god-lists comes a second triad of divinities with an associated female deity. This triad was composed of Sin, the moon-god, Shamash, the sun-god, and Adad, or Hadad, the storm-god, while the associated female figure was that of the goddess Ishtar. Sin is thought to be of nomadic origin, and in early Arabian cult the moon is masculine, while the sun is feminine. Although, since the name Sin is Semitic, the invading Semites may have brought the cult of the moon-god with them, nevertheless he is found in the early Sumerian lists under the name Nannar. While he is called the son of Enlil in the Sumerian lists, his genealogy is not carried back further, and he seems to occupy an independent place among the early Meso-

potamian gods. The phases of the moon were of special importance in the cult, and the period of darkness had the distinctive
name of *bubbulu*; it was thought to be a time when evil spirits
were particularly dangerous. Sin was regarded as the lord of the
calendar, by whom days, months, and years were fixed; but he
was also a vegetation-god, and to him the fertility of cattle was
ascribed. His sacred number was naturally 30, and his emblem
was the crescent. His beard was of lapis lazuli, and on the relief
of Maltaia he is represented as riding on his sacred beast, the
winged bull. Ur and Harran were the two chief centers of his
cult in Mesopotamia. His consort was Ningal, the mother of
the sun-god.

As day was thought to succeed night in the Oriental way of
regarding their relation, the next god in the triad, Shamash, the
sun-god, was thought of as the son of Sin. Here again, while the
cult of the sun-god may have been brought into Mesopotamia by
the invading Semites, since Shamash is a Semitic name, he is also
found in the early Sumerian lists under the name of Babbar, or
Utu.

Shamash is frequently represented on Babylonian seals as
rising from the mountains with rays coming out of his shoulders,
while at night he was thought to descend again through the
mountain gates and to traverse the underworld either on foot,
or in a chariot drawn by fiery mules. He was worshiped by all
classes of people, and his special function was that of upholder
of truth and justice in the life of the community. On the stele
which contains the famous Code of Hammurabi, Shamash is
represented as giving the Laws to the king. Together with Adad
he was regarded as specially concerned with the giving and interpretation of oracles. His sacred number was 20, and the usual
symbol by which he is represented on seals and monuments is
the solar disk with a four-pointed star inside it and rays emerg-
ing from between the points of the star. In Assyria his symbol,
which seems to have been also a symbol of royalty, was a winged
disk, closely resembling the Egyptian winged solar disk. The

chief seat of the cult of Shamash in northern Babylonia was Sippar, and in south Babylonia Larsa. In Ashur he shared a temple with Sin.

The third figure in the triad, Adad, the storm-god, is a divinity whose cult was very widely spread throughout Asia Minor, Mesopotamia, Syria and Palestine. Among the Hittites he bore the name of Teshub; in Syria he was variously known as Resheph, Hadad, and, in the Old Testament, Rimmon. In the earlier stages of Hebrew religion, Yahweh is a storm-god with attributes resembling those of Hadad, and it is not surprising that in northern Israel in the period of the Omri dynasty it was easy for the common people to confuse the attributes of Hadad and Yahweh. Adad is mentioned by Gudea as the "Thunderer," but the general spread of his cult in Babylonia seems to have been the result of closer relations between Babylonia and the west. As the storm-god, Adad is represented as taking a prominent part in the storm which caused the Flood. His sacred number was 6, and the most characteristic symbol of his activities was the lightning which he is generally represented as grasping in his right hand while his left holds an axe. His sacred animal was the bull, a symbol which was very widely dispersed throughout the ancient Near East.

Adad had temples in Babylon and Borsippa, and in Ashur he shared with Anu a ziqqurat which was originally devoted to him alone. He possessed a famous temple in Aleppo, at which offerings were made by various Assyrian kings in the course of their campaigns in Syria. Shalmanezer III, in his "Bull" inscription, records such an offering made to Adad at Aleppo during a campaign in his sixth year.

The female divinity associated with the second triad is the best known and most widely worshiped goddess in the whole Babylonian and Assyrian pantheon, the goddess Ishtar. The usual form of her name in Sumerian is Innina. Although she is, as already stated, associated with the second triad of gods, yet, at an early date, she ousted Anu's legitimate consort, the colorless figure Antu, from her place, and became herself the consort of the high God Anu. She gradually came to absorb into herself the attributes of most of the other female divinities, and was known as "the goddess" par excellence.

She figures largely in Babylonian mythology, especially in the Flood stories and the Epic of Gilgamesh, of which we shall have more to say later. Ishtar presents two very distinct aspects. On the one hand she is the goddess of love and procreation, and those sacred persons known as "hierodules," or temple prostitutes, were attached to her temples; on the other hand, she was also the goddess of war, especially in Assyria, and is figured on seals as armed with bow and quiver; she is even represented as bearded like the god Ashur. In Babylonian astrology her heavenly body was the planet Dilbat, or Venus, and the Bowstar, or Sirius, was also assigned to her. Her sacred number was 15, i.e., half of her father Sin's sacred number. Her symbol was an eight- or sixteen-pointed star. She is generally represented as riding on, or accompanied by, her sacred beast, the lion, though, as on the Ishtar gate of Babylon, she is also associated with the dragon from, the *mushrussu*.

As might be expected, there were many cities where Ishtar was worshiped and had her temples, but her chief center was Erech where her temple staff comprised both male and female hierodules. Here she was worshiped as the Mother-goddess, and as the goddess of love and procreation. Other centers of her cult were Ashur, Babylon, Calah, Ur, Nineveh, and Arbela; in the last-mentioned city she was pre-eminently the goddess of war.

A figure closely connected with Ishtar, but whose place and rank in the pantheon is obscure, is the ancient Sumerian god Tammuz. His Sumerian name, Dumu-zi, means "true son." In the Babylonian king-lists, among the kings who reigned "before the Flood" we find the name of Dumuzi, the Shepherd, while, after the Flood, among the kings of the first dynasty of Erech, immediately preceding Gilgamesh, is Dumuzi, the Fisher. It is difficult to say whether these two figures were originally one. In the numerous Tammuz liturgies, we find preserved the myth of the descent of Tammuz into the underworld, the mourning of Ishtar for her brother-spouse, the descent of Ishtar into the underworld in search of Tammuz, and the triumphant return to earth of the two divinities, bringing back joy and fertility with the spring. It is clear that Tammuz plays the part of a vegetation-god, dying with the dying year and reborn with the spring flowers and the young corn. In the later development of the cult in Babylonia, the myth and ritual of the dying and rising god became stereotyped as the great Babylonian New Year Festival, of which we shall have more to say later. But while the cult of Tammuz ceased to be a state cult in Babylonia and Assyria, it was preserved among the common people, and passed into Syria and Canaan. In Syria he was identified with Adonis, and as late as the beginning of the sixth century B.C. we find in Israel that the ritual weeping for Tammuz was still being practiced by the women. (Ezek. 8:14.)

Associated with Tammuz is his friend and companion, Ningizzida, one of the lesser gods of the underworld. In the myth of Adapa (p. 68f.) Tammuz and Ningizzida are represented as guardians of the gate of the heaven of Anu, but they are also found together as gods of the underworld.

An important group of deities belonging to the underworld must now be mentioned. It is a common possibility that gods of the underworld are the gods of an earlier stage of development, or belonging to a subject population, and the fact that the underworld gods occupy the last place in the god-lists may lend support to this view.

The ruler of the underworld, usually called "the land of no-return" in Babylonian religious texts, was the formidable goddess Ereshkigal, the Semitic form of whose name was Allatu. According to Babylonian mythology, it happened that Ereshkigal summoned Nergal to answer before her for not standing up in the assembly of the gods before her messenger, Namtar.

When Nergal appeared before her he seized her by the hair and dragged her from her throne, intending to cut off her head; thereupon the goddess yielded and proposed that Nergal should become her consort; he accepted the proposal and henceforth shared the dominion of the underworld with Ereshkigal. In his form as a god of the upper world, Nergal seems to have been one aspect of Shamash, representing the sinister side of the sun-god's activities, sending plague, war, devastation and flood. He was believed to spend half the year in the underworld and the other half in the upper world. Cuthah was the principal cult-center of both Ereshkigal and Nergal, but the latter was widely worshiped throughout Mesopotamia, and had temples in Larsa, Isin, and Ashur.

Ereshkigal's messenger, the god Namtar, occurs frequently in the magical texts. He was the herald of death, and in his train were sixty diseases which he had power to let loose upon mankind. A god often associated with Nergal was Irra, the plague-god, a deadly enemy of mankind. As a protection against his activities an incantation tablet was often buried under houses.

These are among the most important deities found in the early Babylonian lists. But there are other gods, not belonging to these lists, of whom mention must be made. First, there is the chief god of Assyria, Ashur, of whose name variant forms appear in early texts: it is found written as A-sir, A-usar, A-shar, with other variants; hence a connection with the name Osiris has been suggested. The form Ashar occurs as the name of an Amorite god, while in the Sumerian liturgies one of the names of Tammuz is recorded as Usir. It has also been claimed that the name of the god is derived from the name of his city, Ashur. Hence it is impossible to give any certain derivation for the name. In Assyria, Ashur assumed the roles of Enlil and Marduk and was also, as might be expected, specially the god of war. One of his commonest symbols was the winged disk inclosing the upper part of the god in the act of discharging an arrow from his bow. We have already seen that Ishtar was regarded in

Assyria as the consort of Ashur, and held the highest place among female deities. Another god whose name is found in Assyrian texts is Shulmanu, who seems to be the Assyrian form of Ninurta.

An interesting group of very ancient gods, excluded from the official list because of their hostility to the Anu heaven of gods, consisted of Tiamat, the chaos-goddess, represented in dragon form, together with her consort, Kingu, and Apsu, the god of the underworld ocean. These three play an important part in the Epic of Creation (p. 6off.).

One of the titles given to Anu, and later to Marduk and Ashur, was "King of the Igigi," while Enlil was styled "King of the Anunnaki." These two terms Igigi and Anunnaki appear to be collective terms designating the gods of heaven, earth, and the underworld, as contained in the official lists, but the two terms seem to be interchangeable. For instance, in a hymn to Sin, we have the words, "When thy voice resounds in heaven the Igigi cast themselves down upon their faces; when thy voice resounds on earth the Anunnaki kiss the ground." Here the Igigi appear to be assigned to heaven and the Anunnaki to earth. On the other hand, we have a text in which the Anunnaki of heaven are stated to be 300 in number. Also the numbers of the Igigi and the Anunnaki vary considerably in different sources. In some texts we hear of eight Igigi and nine Anunnaki, while in others we have 300 Igigi and 600 Anunnaki.

It is often difficult to draw the line between gods and demons; Namtar, for instance, is included in the list as a god, but is also found among the seven evil *utukki*, or demons, often mentioned in exorcism tablets. Demons, some good, but mostly evil, played a large part in the daily life of the Babylonians, and were conceived of in realistic fashion as possessing distinctive forms and individual names. In the reign of Ashurbanipal, a scribe, writing to his royal master, reports that he has caused to be prepared "a picture of Anu's daughter (Lamashtu), a picture of Namtaru, a picture of Latarak, and a picture of Death." Such pictures or figurines were used for protective purposes, either on tablets placed in houses, or as figures buried under thresholds. A familiar Babylonian object was an apotropaic or protective tablet containing on one side an exorcism against the much dreaded female demon Lamashtu, and on the other side a representation of the demon ascending from the underworld to attack her victim. Many of these representations show nightmare forms, part human and part bestial. Unlike the Egyptian conception of their deities, who are frequently represented under theriomorphic forms, the Babylonian and Assyrian gods are always shown in human form, though they are often accompanied by their sacred beasts. This may be due to the fact that Babylonians and their predecessors the Sumerians did not pass through a totemistic stage of religious development, as we know the Egyptians did.

It would be possible to devote a much larger space to the description of the Babylonian pantheon, but the principal figures have been delineated, and it may be said that many of the vast number of gods who compose the pantheon are little more than names. Many of the lesser gods, and some even of the greater ones, are simply personifications of the same attribute, or of the same natural phenomenon, under different names. Many gods are clearly nothing more than personifications of abstract ideas; for example, the consort of Nebo, the god of writing, has the name Tashmetu, which means "Hearing," while, in some early Babylonian religious texts, Ea is represented as having created a goddess called Zaltu, "Strife," as a counterpart to the violence of Ishtar. Further, we can see from the religious literature that a continuous process of merging the attributes of various deities in a single god was going on, especially in the later period of Babylonian religious development. A well-known example is the enumeration of the fifty names of Marduk in the hymn to Marduk which was sung in the New Year Festival, where Marduk has absorbed the attributes of many other gods, and in one interesting hymn the various bodily parts of Nergal are represented as equated with other gods, thus, "His eyes are Enlil and Ninlil, Sin is the pupil of his eyes, Anu and Entu are his lips, his teeth are the Sibittu (the seven gods), his ears are Ea and Damkina, his skull is Adad, his neck is Marduk, and his breast is Nebo."

Nevertheless, it can be seen from Babylonian penitential hymns that a sense of personal relationship with the god, and of something not wholly unlike the experience of guilt and estrangement found in the Hebrew Psalter, was present in Babylonian religious experience, at least in its later stages. (See p. 98.)

Before leaving the subject of the Babylonian pantheon there is one aspect of Babylonian theology which should be briefly discussed, namely, the question of divine kingship in Babylonia and Assyria. In the first place, it must be remarked that an important distinction exists between kingship in Egypt and kingship in Mesopotamia, a distinction which has not been sufficiently recognized in earlier books on this subject. This has been very clearly brought out by Professor Frankfort, especially in the book already mentioned, *Kingship and the Gods*. In Egypt the Pharaoh was from the beginning identified with Re, the creator and sun-god; after death he was equated with the god Osiris, while his successor was equated with the god Horus. From the beginning to the end of Egyptian history the Pharaoh was unequivocally divine and was treated as a god.

In Mesopotamia the situation was more ambiguous. A number of Mesopotamian kings have the divine determinative prefixed to their names (in cuneiform the determinative sign indicating deity is an eight-pointed star), chiefly in the early period. A notable case is that of Naram-sin who has the divine determinative before his name, and on his famous stele is represented as larger than human (like the Egyptian convention), and as wearing the horned cap characteristic of the gods. In a well-known Tammuz liturgy[1] we have the names of eleven kings of Ur and

[1] M. Witzel, *Tammuz-liturgien und Verwandtes*, 17.

27

Isin with the divine determinative, and in the New Year Festival the king represented the god in several important ritual situations, especially the sacred marriage. Professor Frankfort, who, as already shown, derives the institution of kingship from the "primitive democracy," explains the divine character of kingship from the element of the sacred marriage in Babylonian ritual. These are his words:

"It may well be that only those kings were deified who had been commanded by a goddess to share her couch. In a general way the kings who use the divine determinative before their names belong to the same period as the texts mentioning the marriage of kings and goddesses; and we have seen that some kings adopted the determinative, not at the beginning, but at a later stage of their reigns. If we assume that they did so on the strength of a divine command, we remain within the normal scope of Mesopotamian thought, while the view that a king should have presumed of his own accord to pass the barrier between the human and the divine conflicts with everything we know of Mesopotamian beliefs."[2] Professor Frankfort goes on to use another well-known early text, "The Deification of Lipit-ishtar," to support his theory. This text is an actual deification ritual in which the king Lipit-ishtar is identified with the fertility god Urash as a preliminary to his marriage with the goddess Ishtar. This text has been used, perhaps without due limitation, to support the view that divine kingship was an essential element in Babylonian religion. Professor Frankfort has shown that such a view needs considerable modification, but it is possible that the last word has not yet been said about this perplexing problem. If we substitute the term "sacral" for divine, it may be permissible to claim that, whatever its origin, kingship in Mesopotamia and in the lands influenced by Mesopotamian ideas and practices developed a sacral character in connection with ritual at a very early period, a character which was maintained and

---

[2] Frankfort, *op. cit.*, 297.

intensified until the end of that civilization which had given birth to the idea.

EXCURSUS ON TAMMUZ

Although Tammuz does not play a large part in the state rituals of Babylonia or Assyria, as we have seen in the previous chapter, yet it is clear that his cult must have belonged to an early stage of Mesopotamian religion and spread widely beyond the boundaries of Babylonia. His cult is mentioned in the Old Testament, and its influence is to be found in the Ras Shamra texts. Hence a somewhat fuller account of that cult and the connected literature is added here in an excursus.

There is only one explicit reference to the cult of Tammuz in the Old Testament, namely, the well-known passage in Ezek. 7:14, in which the prophet describes his vision of the women of Jerusalem weeping for Tammuz at the north gate of the Temple at Jerusalem. An indirect reference may be found in Isa. 17:10, where the words *nit‘e na‘amanim* are usually interpreted as referring to the "gardens of Adonis," a feature of the Phoenician form of the Tammuz cult.

But in recent years much fresh material relating to this cult has been made available for study. This is to be found in M. Witzel's *Tammuz-liturgien und Verwandtes*, a collection of over seventy liturgies belonging to the central ritual of the Tammuz cult; also in Ebeling's *Tod und Leben nach den Vorstellungen der Babylonier*, a collection of thirty-seven ritual texts of various kinds, many of which represent later developments of the Tammuz cult. Reference may also be made to earlier collections, such as Zimmern's *Tammuz Lieder*, Langdon's *Babylonian Liturgies*, and de Genouillac's *Textes religieux sumériens*. A valuable discussion of the subject is to be found in Frankfort's *Kingship and the Gods*, already referred to in the previous chapter.

There are two main types of literature to be dealt with:

a) The great liturgies, which give us a picture of the Tammuz ritual and its associated myth.

b) Magical texts, representing later developments of the ritual in its application to the needs of individuals.

Taking the first body of material, we find that there is, in spite of minor variations, a close general resemblance between the liturgies which have survived in a complete form. The main outlines are clear. The usual opening contains a description of the woe and desolation which have fallen upon the temple, city, and people, as the result of the triumph of the demonic powers of the underworld over Tammuz, the shepherd of his people. Then follows the summons to universal mourning. Ishtar, the mother, sister and consort of Tammuz, calls upon priests and people to unite with her in lamentation. The lament appears to be an echo of the "word" or cry of Tammuz himself from the underworld. The "word" has magic power, and brings destruction, irrevocable until the god himself has recalled his "word." The laments, antiphonal in character, go on to describe the destruction of the temple, the wasting of the land with its inhabitants and its produce, under the raging storm of the onset of the powers of the underworld, "the blast of the terrible one," a phrase of continual recurrence in the laments. The laments describe with great detail the sad condition of the captive god, bound in the underworld, in "the steppe," fallen into a magic sleep, lying among withered vegetation, scorched with fiery heat. They continue with the description of the sorrows of Ishtar, she is like a wife bereft of her husband, a mother bereft of her child, a cow of its calf, a goat of its kid, a sheep of its lamb.

The laments, accompanied with ritual actions, occupy the main part of the liturgy. Then comes the ritual consultation of the underworld oracle by Ishtar, and her announcement of her decision to descend into the underworld to seek her husband. This is accompanied by a description of the ceremonial adornment of the goddess in preparation for her journey. She says that she has painted her eyes with stibium for him, that she has decked her shoulders with boughs of sweet-smelling cedar, her body with shining robes, and her head with a gleaming diadem for him.

Then comes a cry from the underworld, from the vanished Tammuz, for propitiatory offerings and the preparation of a ritual banquet. After the preparation of the feast comes the description of a ceremonial procession of deified kings whose names are given, namely those from Ur-Nammu, the first king of the third dynasty of Ur, (2294 B.C.) to Pur-Sin, the seventh king of the Isin dynasty (2040 B.C.),[3] giving us an approximate period for these early liturgies, slightly earlier than the time of Hammurabi.

As each king approaches with his gifts he utters the refrain, "Rejoice thine heart with thy vegetation." Then Ishtar says, "Led by the voice of the oracle, I come to thee," and invokes Tammuz by all his titles, ending with the words, "To thee, my wild bull in the steppe, my lamb in the steppe, will I direct my prayer." Once more Ishtar declares that she has decked herself like a cedar to make glad the heart of him, her child, her beloved, who has passed over the river. Then comes the final song of triumph which begins, "Calling to the Lord, thou hast delivered thy noble cedar tree from prison." The end appears to be a doxology addressed to the reunited gods in the bridal chamber.

The first suggestion to be made in connection with this liturgical material is that it represents a very early stage of Mesopotamian religion, probably much earlier than the more elaborate ritual of the Babylonian New Year Festival to which it has largely contributed. It is well known that the cult of Adonis had an important place in the religion of northern Syria, and the many points of resemblance between the Tammuz liturgies and the Ras Shamra texts tend to strengthen the grounds for the view that the Tammuz cult formed part of the general early religious

[3] This is the date given by Sidney Smith in his *Early History of Assyria* (1928) but as the dates for this period have been considerably lowered, it may be a couple of centuries later.

background of the Near East. Further, while urban development and political changes in Mesopotamia led to changes in the form of the central ritual of the state, obscuring its original agricultural and fertility characteristics to some extent, Canaan and Syria may have retained much of the earlier and simpler character of the Tammuz cult.

It is with such a form of the Tammuz cult as the Ras Shamra texts represent that the early Hebrew settlers would come into contact, and it is also possible that the element of Hebrew settlement which came from Mesopotamia may have preserved the memory of the general character and style of the Tammuz liturgies. There are a number of passages in Hebrew poetic literature which suggest, not direct borrowing, but the influence of certain literary forms. It is not possible to do more here than indicate some of the more striking parallels in style.

There are several vivid passages in the liturgies which describe the destruction of the temples of Tammuz. Langdon thinks that such descriptions refer to historical events, but it is possible that there was a ritual destruction of the sacred buildings as part of the proceedings in the annual ceremonies connected with the disappearance of Tammuz. In these passages we hear of the destruction of the pillars and carved work of the temple, of the profanation of the sanctuary into which no foot had entered, of the breaking through of the enemy into the sacred enclosure of cedar trees, and of the scattering of the slain corpses of the people in the courts of the holy place. Coupled with such descriptions there is the plaint that natural affection has ceased, that the mother has ceased to care for her children, and the father for his young; that the holy throne has been removed from the sanctuary, and that the Lord who gives counsel and response from the oracle has disappeared.

In Ps. 74:3–9 there is a vivid description of the destruction of the temple which presents remarkably close parallels with the descriptions of the ruin wrought in the temples of Tammuz by the underworld powers. The rather difficult verse 5, "they made themselves known as men that lifted up axes upon a thicket of trees," may find an explanation in the description of the enemy in the Tammuz liturgies as breaking through the inclosure of sacred cedars.

Again, the description of the Scythian invasions in Jer. 6:23–29, 9:19–22, and other passages, bears a very close resemblance to the descriptions of the wasting of the city and the land, before the raging storm of fire and burning wind from the steppes, in the liturgies with which we are concerned.

Another type of literary resemblance is found between such descriptions as those in Isa. 14:9–19, Ezek. 32:20–31, with its refrain, and the descriptions of the fallen and miserable state of the god who has been cast out like refuse, and has gone down into the pit, held captive by demonic powers.

This line of comparison might be pursued considerably further, but its general effect is to suggest that the early and widespread prevalence of these liturgies in Mesopotamia and the lands subject to its cultural influence provided a stock of poetic forms and imagery available for use when an appropriate occasion called for them. It is not suggested that Hebrew prophets, or the composers of canticles for sacred occasions, borrowed directly from Mesopotamian sources, but that they made use of ancient poetic forms and metaphors where they could be adapted to the expression of the new religious ideas growing out of their own religious experience.

This is only in keeping with what is acknowledged to have taken place in other cultural spheres, in the domain of law and of ritual, for example.

There are two other points of contact which arise out of the liturgies. One, already alluded to, is the special significance attached to the "word" of Tammuz. As he goes down into the underworld the god is represented as pronouncing woe upon his city and his land. All the tribulations which the land and people suffer, the letting loose of the storm from the underworld, and even the things which the god himself suffers, are conceived as the result of the magic potency of the "word." Until Tammuz himself takes back his word, neither prayer nor spell can avail to turn aside the course of events. But when the god awakes out of his magic sleep, the first thing which happens is the uttering of his voice, he roars like a wild bull, and the reversal of the fortunes of the land begins, together with the return of the god to his temple. In the language used of the "word" of Tammuz and its effects, with the emphasis on the impossibility of turning it back, also in the various metaphors employed to describe the voice of the god, we find a similar close analogy with the language used by Hebrew poets to describe both the devastating effects of Yahweh's word when he is angry, and the refreshing effects in rain and verdure of his word in mercy. We also hear of Yahweh's awaking out of sleep, roaring like a warrior or a wild animal, and discomfiting his foes. Again the suggestion is not of direct borrowing or imitation, but of the use by Hebrew poets of a *gattung*, a literary form, ready to their hand, to express their own ideas of the activity of Yahweh.

The other point arises out of the relation between Ishtar and Tammuz, and the frequent use of the symbol of the cedar both for the god and the goddess. We shall meet this point again in connection with the magical texts, but here it is a question of the two different aspects of the symbol. In connection with the god there is the ritual element frequently represented on pre-Sargonid seals of the felling of a tree on the sacred mountain to represent the death of the god. Ishtar mourns the loss of her noble cedar tree. This piece of ritual is found in Phoenicia, and the *ded*-tree in Egyptian ritual has the same significance. On the other hand the cedar in its bravery is the symbol which the goddess uses repeatedly to express her own attractiveness as she prepares to meet her risen husband. The sacred pole as the symbol of Ishtar, or Astarte, or any other form of the mother-goddess, is everywhere to be found in the ancient Near East, though the male symbol took the form of the pillar. But in this early stage the cedar represents both the male and female divinity, one fallen and then raised up, for the dying and rising Tammuz, the other in the verdure and sweet smell of its luxuriant branches, for the goddess seeking her husband. It may be suggested that Hos. 14:8, where Ephraim says "I am like a green fir tree," and Yahweh replies "From me is thy fruit found," is a piece of imagery drawn from the same source. Ephraim, as the wife seeking the husband to whom she has been unfaithful, uses the language of Ishtar, "I am a green fir tree," and Yahweh replies in the character of the fruit-giver.

There are many other things in the liturgies which invite discussion as throwing light on obscure phrases and metaphors in the Old Testament, but it is necessary to turn now to the other class of Tammuz texts, namely, the magical texts.

These texts illustrate the principle, well established for Mesopotamian religion, that the great central rituals for the seasonal festivals are essentially magical in character, and that they become the source for all kinds of lesser occasional rituals in which their magic is used for individual needs, such as various kinds of sickness, headache, fevers, epilepsy, etc.

The eleventh text in Ebeling's collection bears the title, "When a man has been attacked by the *utukku*-demon, the *saghulhaza*-demon, or any other evil thing." It goes on to prescribe the ritual for such a case. The first part of the ritual consists of invocations addressed to Ishtar and Tammuz, with other lesser deities, accompanied by offerings of a symbolic character. The first invocation begins, "In the month of Tammuz, when Ishtar causes the people of the lands to weep for Tammuz, her husband, then, when the families of mankind are gathered together there, Ishtar appears and, beholding the situation of mankind, takes away sickness and causes sickness.

"On the twenty-eighth of the month, the day of sheepfolds, thou shalt offer a vulva of lapis lazuli, and a golden star to Ishtar; thou shalt name the name of the sick man, and say, 'Deliver the sick man.' " On the twenty-ninth day a bed is prepared for Tammuz, i.e., a funeral couch, and various offerings of food and drink are brought for the god. Further invocations are addressed to Tammuz and Ishtar, asking that the evil spirits which have attacked the sick man may be driven out of him, and that Tammuz will take them with him into the underworld.

Then comes the prescription of the necessary ritual acts. The sick man must stand at the foot of the funeral couch of Tammuz and cover his face, signifying that he is dead. Then the priest strikes him seven times with a reed, and the instructions add, "As soon as thou hast touched him, he is changed (*ramanšu ušpil*)." The nature of the change implied appears from the words which immediately follow, "And thus shalt thou say to him, 'May Ishtar, thy beloved, go by thy side' "; that is, the sick man has exchanged his own personality for that of the god. The sick man then leaves the foot of the bed, puts on sackcloth, wounds himself, kneels before Ishtar and prays, "Ishtar, save thy people (or, possibly, thy man, i.e., thy husband)." The priest is then to cut off the forelock from the sick man's head, and remove his girdle, and to cast them into the river (the symbol of the underworld), with twelve loaves and a measure of fine meal. This, so to speak, completes the exchange of personality. The sick man then abstains from certain food and wears sackcloth for three days, i.e., the period during which Tammuz is in the underworld. With this the ritual is complete. The efficacy of it consists in the exchange of personality, by which the sickness is transferred to the god, the sick man symbolically dies and rises with the god and is freed from the power of the evil spirit.

This text illustrates clearly the principle of the *puhu-* or substitution-ritual, of which various forms are given in other texts in the same collection. We have the case of the death of Shamashshumukin which is referred to in Harper's Assyrian and Babylonian Letters, No. 437, as a substitutionary death for his rebellious nobles. There is also the *sar-puhi*, the substitute king in the later period of the history of the New Year Festival. In other magical texts relating to the ritual for curing various diseases caused by the presence of evil spirits we find the same principle expressed in different ways. In one text a kid, a familiar symbol of Tammuz, is the sick man's substitute. The sick man is killed in symbol with a wooden dagger, while the kid is ritually slain with a copper dagger; the kid is then treated as a dead person, embalmed, mourned and buried with proper rites, and the sick man recovers. Other forms of substitute are a pig (also found in the New Year ritual), a lamb, a clay image of the sick man or of the evil spirit, and even a rat.

One particularly interesting example of the *puhu*-ritual may be cited, and it will serve to carry us on to the question of the origin of the substitutionary element in the Hebrew ritual system. This is a text which deals with the case of a man with a dumb spirit, i.e., some form of aphasia, or perhaps, more accurately, paralysis of the throat muscles. The ritual prescribed was as follows: a kid was tied to the head of the sick man's bed, a stick was cut from the garden and wrapped in colored wool, a jar filled with water, and a cedar cut from the garden. Then the stick, the jar and the cedar were placed for the night in a place called *abulli ša darati* (gate of eternity), of which the meaning is not clear. In the morning the kid, the stick, the jar of water, and the cedar were brought to the edge of the desert, already explained as the symbol of the underworld. The stick and the jar of water are left there, but the kid and the cedar are taken to a crossroad; there the kid is killed, skinned, the head cut off, but the limbs left attached to the hide; the flesh is cooked, the hide of the kid is wrapped round the cedar, funerary offerings of honey and oil are placed in pots, a hole is dug, the honey and oil poured in, and the cedar wrapped in the hide of the kid is buried therein. The sick man eats of the cooked flesh. The last line, unfortunately broken, seems to have said that on the day when some unspecified person or thing rose again the sick man would be freed from his incubus and his mouth be opened.

Here the principle of substitution is somewhat elaborate, but sufficiently clear. The kid is Tammuz and the cedar may be either Tammuz or Ishtar, probably the latter; they are symbolically buried in the desert, the sick man is identified with Tammuz as fully as possible, and the final result is the removal of his disease.

The comparison is obvious with the substitutionary element in the Hebrew ritual of the Day of Atonement, namely, the goat for Azazel that is sent away into the wilderness. In the light of the parallels from the magical texts the only satisfactory explanation of the name Azazel seems to be that which takes it as the name of some demon, while the desert has the same symbolic meaning as in the Tammuz liturgies and magical texts, namely, the underworld.

But the parallel raises the question of the origin of the different aspects of Hebrew sacrificial ritual. In the later developments of the Tammuz ritual as we see it in the magical texts, three associated conceptions appear in connection with the death of the victim. First there is the idea already discussed, the victim is a symbol of the god, and by identification of the offerer with the victim a transference of the offerer's sickness or guilt to the symbol of the god is effected. The offerer partakes symbolically in the suffering and death and resurrection of the god, and thereby obtains deliverance. Secondly, the idea of placation is present; the hostile powers of the underworld are supposed to be satisfied by the substitute, we have the phrase "*a puhu for Ereshkigal*," just as we have the Hebrew expression "one goat for Azazel." Thirdly, the idea has arisen that the carcass of the victim or its blood may serve as a means of purification, either for a sacred building, as in the New Year ritual, or for an individual.

This is not the place to begin a discussion on the general theory of the origin of sacrifice among the Semites, but the suggestion may be permitted, as germane to the material dealt with, that there are two main lines along which the institution of sacrifice developed, each arising from a different source. There is the group of sacrifices expressing in various ways the three main ideas of substitution, placation and purification, a group which embraces the most important types of Hebrew sacrifice, the *'olah, kalil,' 'asham, hata'ath*, and there is also the group of offerings coming under the general name of *minhah* and *mattanah*. The former group may be traced back to developments from the early rituals connected with the death of a god, rituals which were central in the early stages of religion in the Near East. The second group, it is suggested, arose out of the conception of the god as the owner of the land, possessing a dwelling place, and surrounded by an organized body of priests and temple servants. The god's title was recognized by the bringing of offerings from the flocks and herds, and from the fruits of the soil, and the fiction was kept up that the gods needed their daily meals.

In Thureau-Dangin's collection of Akkadian rituals, we find provision made for the "great meal" and the "little meal," *petit déjeuner*, so to speak, and in this way the maintenance of the temple staffs was secured. We have lists of animals, birds, wine, beer, oil, bread, and everything necessary for the table of the gods. One of the earliest tablets from Ras Shamra to be deciphered contained such a list. The principle was capable of large extension, and hence arose a class of offerings unconnected with the three main ideas of substitution, placation and purification. Such offerings were gifts, not exactly voluntary, but arising from the nature of the relation between the god and the worshiper, and intended to maintain that relation in a satisfactory state.

Hence, while Buchanan Gray is right when he points out that none of the specific Hebrew terms except *nedarim* imply the idea of a gift to the god, it seems clear that historically all the specific types of offering belong to one or other of two main classes, whether they are slain, burnt, eaten in part by the offerer, or merely presented in the presence of the god. They are either offerings which have their origin in the central rite of the death of the god and the ideas connected therewith, or they are in essence gifts, given no doubt in recognition of the due claims of the god and his entourage, but, even though they may aim at securing the favor of the god, still retaining the character of gifts.

CHAPTER IV

TEMPLE BUILDINGS AND PERSONNEL

IN the previous chapter it has been shown that the principal gods of the Babylonian pantheon had cities which were the special centers of their cult. Thus Babylon was the city where Marduk held the chief place among the other gods who were worshiped there; Shamash, the sun-god, had his seat at Sippar, while the moon-god Sin was worshiped at Ur and Harran. In these local centers the god had his own house, called by the Sumerians the "Great House" (E. GAL), which formed the center of a complex of temple buildings, varying in size according to the importance of the god and the wealth of the city. In these buildings lived the temple staff of priests and priestesses who performed all the various functions pertaining to the worship of the god and the administration of his estates. It is the purpose of this chapter to give a description of the Babylonian or Assyrian temple and its staff of priests.

The Temple. Excavation has shown that in the great cities, such as Babylon or Ur, the temple buildings were very elaborate and occupied a large extent of ground. But in the early stages of the growth of the cult the place where the image of the god was housed and the priest was consulted might be a very small and humble affair, indeed nothing more than a mud and reed hut. We have a representation of such a simple shrine on the well-known pictographic tablet from Kish. A very early alabaster relief in the British Museum shows a reed hut with the two reed bundles which are the insignia of the Mother-goddess Innina; the hut is a sacred sheep pen, and may be regarded as an early type of sacred building. But by the end of the third millennium B.C. the simple shrine had developed into an extensive group of buildings of which the temple itself was the center, surrounded by side chapels for the lesser gods, priests' rooms, kitchens, schoolrooms, libraries, slaughterhouses, and many other rooms for various purposes connected with the worship and service of the god. In the larger cities there were many temples; for example, according to contemporary documents and descriptive lists, there were in Babylon in the time of Nebuchadnezzar II no less than fifty-eight temples belonging to designated gods, to say nothing of many other temples not so assigned. Hence it can be seen how large a part the priestly caste must have played in the life of a great city.

The sites of many temples in Babylonia and Assyria have been excavated during the last half-century, and it can be seen that temples varied considerably in plan. But they all possessed a central court and a *cella* or chamber in which there was a niche and pedestal for the statue of the god. The larger and more important temples would have lesser courts surrounded by rooms for the priests to robe in, storerooms, and rooms for various purposes. The plan of the temple of Gula in Babylon may serve as an example of the layout of a typical temple. It consists of a rectangular enclosure, orientated northwest and southeast, as befitted a goddess of the underworld, since the underworld was part of the domain of Ea, the lord of Ocean, which the Babylonians located in the Persian Gulf to the southeast of Babylon.

The temple contained a large central court and two lesser courts opening from it on the west side. The main door of the temple and the main entrance to the central court, called by the Babylonians the *kisalmahhu*, or "sublime court," were on the north. On entering the main door the worshiper had a blank wall in front of him, and it was not until he had passed through the forecourt and entered the vestibule, that he could see through the main court the approach to the antechamber and the niche, where the statue of the goddess stood. On a feast day the procession of worshipers and priests would enter the main gate, pass through the forecourt and vestibule into the central court, enter the antechamber and deposit the gifts they brought before the goddess in her *cella*; then the procession would pass out by a corridor on the east side of the antechamber, up a narrow passage northwards and out by the side door on the east, thus avoiding confusion with the entrants. Each of the two lesser courts was surrounded by living rooms and smaller rooms forming the dwelling place of the chief priest and his assistants. The goddess Gula was much sought after as a healer, and the elaborate arrangement of corridors and side-chambers suggests provision for the attendance of the sick and for the ministrations of the priests. We shall deal in a later chapter with the rituals and incantations which the priests used in the treatment of disease.

The largest and most splendid of Babylonian temples was, naturally, that of Marduk, the tutelary god of Babylon. Its Babylonian name was Esagila, "the house that lifts up its head." It was a vast quadrangular inclosure on the east bank of the Euphrates, surrounded by high turreted walls. In the northern part of the great court was the *ziqqurat*, the temple tower, commonly known as "the Tower of Babel," of which more will be said later; in the southern half of the court was the temple of Marduk, with its fifty-five side chapels. The Sacred Way, or processional street passed up the west side of the temple, on which lay the four great gates by which processions entered and left the sacred inclosure. Within the temple Esagila were the chapels of Zarpanit, Marduk's consort, Nebo his son, Ea the god of wisdom and the Ocean, Nusku the Fire-god, Tashmetu the goddess of Hearing (i.e., hearing prayer), and various other gods and goddesses. Babylonian and Assyrian kings had vied with each other in enriching the great shrine with gifts. When Esagila was rebuilt in the reign of Esarhaddon, that king made gifts of silver and gold vessels to the value of fifty minas; the statue of Marduk, his table, chair, and footstool, were of solid gold, and weighed eighty talents. The "golden heaven," which had a part in the ceremonies of the New Year Festival at Babylon, was a baldachin or canopy of gold or cloth of gold upon which the planets were represented. In the cylinders of Gudea, an early priest-king of Lagash, we read of the costly materials which were used in the building of E-ninnu, the temple of Ninurta; gold, lapis lazuli, marble, alabaster, cedarwood; other rare woods were brought from Elam, Magan, and Meluhha; large numbers of craftsmen, goldsmith, and stonemasons were gathered, and the description of the work bears an interesting resemblance to that of the building of Solomon's temple at Jerusalem. Two kinds of sacred buildings are of special interest and call for some description:

The ziqqurat. This remarkable feature of the complex of temple buildings has been found in most of the ancient city sites excavated in Mesopotamia. The form of the ziqqurat varied in different localities, but its general pattern was that of a great rectangular tower, rising by diminishing stages to a summit on which there was a chapel, originally perhaps a temporary wooden structure, in which the ritual of the sacred marriage was celebrated. The different stages were reached by external ramps or stairways. Underneath the building was a chamber, sometimes called *gigunu*, about the purpose of which scholars are not wholly in agreement, but which may have been used for some important part of the New Year ritual. The ziqqurat was not, like the Egyptian pyramid, a royal tomb, but the tradition that it was the tomb of Bel may have arisen from its use as the place where the dead body of the god lay concealed before his resurrection at the central moment of the New Year Festival at Babylon. It is certain that the ziqqurat was not, in the strict sense, a temple, i.e., the abode of a god, but it was a sacred building and played a most important part in the great Babylonian rituals. Behind the Hebrew story of the purpose of the Tower of Babel there lies the fact that the ancient Babylonians regarded the ziqqurat as in some way a bond between heaven and earth; it is possible that the seven stages of Etemenanki, the ziqqurat of Babylon, may have had astrological significance.

The akitu was a special temple, usually separate from the central complex of temple buildings, which played an important part in the ceremonial of the New Year Festival. It was the place to which, on the tenth day of the Festival, the sacred procession, headed by Marduk, made its way from Esagila in order to carry out some essential part of the New Year ritual.

We must now turn to consider the nature and functions of the temple personnel.

The Priesthood. In the early period of the city-states of Sumer and Akkad, the city-ruler, called in Sumerian the *patesi* (or *ensi*), and in Akkadian the *ishshaku*, exercised the double function of priest-king. But in the course of time the priestly function became detached, and a special class of sacred persons came into existence whose business it was to serve as intermediaries between the god and his people. Since the god was regarded as the owner of the land and the people as his tenants, an important part of the priests' duties consisted in the administration of the god's estates and the collection of his rents and dues. The earliest written tablets known to us come from the temple of Ishtar in Erech, and consist of records of such dues paid in kind to the priests. But the duties of the priests who made up the staff of one of the great city temples were manifold, and a list of the various classes of priests will give some idea of the scope of their activities.

There is no word in Akkadian with the meaning "high priest" (unless the title *sangu mah* has this meaning), no doubt because originally the king was head of the religious as well as of the secular activities of his state. But in course of time a priest who bore the title of *urigallu*, and whose original functions are obscure, came to assume the principal place in the priesthood, and we find him performing the central acts in the great seasonal rituals. The following are the names of the main classes of priests as known to us from the various religious texts from Babylonia and Assyria.

i) The *kalû*-priests. This class of priests had as its special province the music of the temple. The function of the kalû-priests was "to appease the heart of the great gods" by the chanting of hymns and liturgies to the accompaniment of musical instruments, the most important of which was the *lilissu*-drum. They are frequently mentioned as taking part in the ceremonies of the New Year Festival.

ii) An important class of priests dealt with that aspect of Babylonian religion which was concerned with the belief in evil spirits and their activities. Such priests bore the names *mashmashu* and *ashipu*, and their function was to protect the individual from the malice of evil spirits by the performance of rituals and the recital of incantations. A pregnant woman was specially exposed to the attacks of evil spirits, and for protection she would call in the *ashipu* who met her need by a ritual of tying sacred knots and reciting appropriate spells. Various forms of common diseases were regarded as due to the activities of evil spirits, and to counteract these the *ashipu* was called in to perform the rituals and recite the incantations which would deliver the sufferer from the power of the evil spirit. As an example of such a ritual we have a text in which it is prescribed that the sick person is to have a kid laid in the bed with him; then they are to strike the sick man's throat with a wooden dagger, and to cut the kid's throat with a copper dagger. Next the kid is clothed with the sick man's clothes, a lament for the dead is raised over it, and funerary offerings are made to Ereshkigal, the goddess of the underworld, while the priest recites the incantation "the great brother i.e., Tammuz) is his brother." Then the sick man will recover. This ritual is an example of an important element in Babylonian religion, the principle of *puhu*, or "substitution"; the kid as a symbol of Tammuz becomes the substitute for the sick person.

iii) A very ancient and important class of priests was that included under the name *barû*, or "seer." The *barû* observed the omens and interpreted dreams. He accompanied the king on campaigns and gave decisions concerning favorable days for beginning an enterprise. The ordering of the calendar, observation of the new moon and of the planets, and indication of lucky and unlucky days, formed part of the duties of the *barû*, and we have frequent mention of his activities in the State correspondence of the Assyrian kings.

iv) The priesthood was not confined to men, but women formed part of the staff of the great temples. It was considered an honor to belong to the order of priestesses, and we hear of several kings who dedicated their daughters to the priestly calling. The Code of Hammurabi lays down rules for their behavior and defines their civil rights. Some of them lived in a special abode or cloister, but in general they were free to move about in society. Their most important function was to serve as sacred prostitutes at the great seasonal festivals. Their Akkadian name, *qadishtu*, corresponds to the Hebrew *qedēshah* who figures in early Hebrew religion. The temple of Ishtar, naturally, contained a large staff of such women, who were known by the special name *ishtaritu*.

With a few exceptions it was the custom for the priesthood to become hereditary, and for the special knowledge of the various priestly functions to be transmitted from father to son; hence there was no rule of celibacy for the Babylonian clergy. The knowledge of the rituals was regarded as a secret to be jealously guarded; at the end of a ritual text there is frequently to be found a colophon in such words as, "The rites which you shall perform may be seen by the novice; the stranger or outsider may not see them, or his days will be cut short. The initiate is to teach them to the initiate; the profane person may not see them; it is among the things forbidden by the great gods, Anu, Enlil, and Ea." The course of training for the priesthood was long and comprehensive; the mere learning of the complicated

47

system of cuneiform writing, and the mastery of Sumerian as the sacred language of the rituals, was by itself a heavy task. The temple singers and instrumentalists underwent a three-year course of training, and it is probable that the higher grades of priests would need a much longer period of instruction.

Early Babylonian seals show that at first it was customary for priests to perform their functions naked, but later on the usual dress of the ministrant was a white linen garment. On certain occasions, however, the priest appeared dressed in a red robe, possibly to inspire fear in evil spirits; for a similar reason animal masks were worn by priests during the performance of apotropaic or protective rituals. The fiction was maintained that the gods ate the offerings of food and drank the offerings of wine, and in the texts we have the detailed menu of the "great breakfast" and the "little breakfast" of the gods, suggesting that they were hearty feeders; but in actuality such offerings of food constituted the maintenance of the priests. We have many texts which prescribe the daily rate of subsistence due to the various grades of priests. There was a wide divergence in this respect between the higher and lower orders of clergy, and the hardworking *ashipu* was very poorly paid in comparison with an *erib biti*, i.e., a priest who had the privilege of entry into the shrine. Plurality of offices was not uncommon, and we hear of a priest in the reign of Shamshu-iluna who was at the same time temple secretary, anointing priest, temple brewer, doorkeeper, and purifier of the temple court, each of which offices carried with it its own salary. The number of priests attached to a temple varied according to the importance both of the city and the god to whom it belonged, but in the great city-temples the staff was very large.

In a list of the temple staff of the goddess Bau in the time of Urukagina, *circ.* 2600 B.C., 736 persons are enumerated, and later, in the great days of the Neo-Babylonian dynasty, the staff of Marduk's temple probably numbered several thousand. It is, perhaps, not surprising to find complaints of the abuse of power

King Ashurbanipal carrying a basket for the rebuilding of Esagila in Babylon. British Museum, London.

Hammurabi (1955–1913 B.C.) receives the law from the hand of the sun-god, Shamash. Louvre, Paris.

and privilege by the priesthood similar to those which we find made by the prophets of Israel. King Urukagina accuses the priests of taking the best of the cattle for themselves, and of robbing the gardens of the poor. At a later date we find a priest charging a colleague with having slanderously accused him to the king of having broken open a sealed chest and stolen precious stones; while a priest of the temple of Ninurta reports to the king that a high official of the temple has removed some of the gold from the golden canopy of the god.

The correspondence of the Assyrian kings shows how large a part the priesthood played in court affairs, and in general the power of the priesthood waxed or waned with the waning or waxing of the civil power of the state. Under the powerful Assyrian kings the influence of the priesthood was strictly limited to its proper sphere, but in Babylon, owing to the pre-eminent place which that city held as the religious capital of Mesopotamia, even after its political importance had declined, the priesthood always exercised great power, especially during the closing days of the Neo-Babylonian empire, whose last king, Nabonidus, was a priest and an appointee of the priestly college. There was, however, one prerogative which the kings of Babylonia and Assyria never surrendered, namely, the right to appoint their own nominees to the higher priestly offices, a right which was often exercised in favor of their own relatives. We learn from the records that Ashurbanipal appointed his two younger brothers as chief priests of Ashur and Sin respectively, while it was not uncommon for the king's daughter to be appointed "lady of the house," i.e., chief priestess. We must now turn to the various services and ritual activities which made up the pattern of the Babylonian religious year, and which may be comprised under the general term "cultus."

49

CHAPTER V

THE RITUALS

W<small>E</small> shall see when we come to deal with the Babylonian Creation myths that they show a considerable variety of forms, but common to nearly all of them is the idea that man was created for *dullu*, i.e., the service of the gods. Such service was conceived of in a very literal and material way. The gods liked eating and drinking, music and dancing; they required beds to sleep in and to enjoy the pleasures of marital intercourse; they had to be washed and dressed, and appeased with pleasant odors; they had to be taken out for drives on state occasions. All such activities assumed the fiction that the images of the gods were alive, but for the ancient Babylonians it was more than a fiction. In the *bit-mummu*, the craftsman's house, where the images were made, before being installed in their shrines they had to undergo certain rituals known as *mis-pi*, "mouth-washing," and *pit-pi*, "opening of the mouth," by which it was believed that they were imbued with life. There is an interesting resemblance between this ritual and the well-known Egyptian ritual called "the opening of the mouth," by which life was imparted to the portrait statues of the dead.

The daily ritual of the temple consisted, in the first place, of the washing, dressing, and feeding of the images of the gods. The shrines were furnished with tables having two steps, on one of which flowers were placed, and on the other the food and drink for the divine participants; there were also censers or braziers in which incense was burned; pure water was sprinkled by the attendant priest to purify the shrine in which the repasts took place. The food offered to the gods consisted of bread and cakes, the flesh of various animals, such as bulls, sheep, goats, deer; fish is mentioned among the articles of diet, and poultry of various kinds.

The killing of animals for the food of the gods, although carried out ritually by a priest whose special duty this was, and who had the title of *nas-patri*, "dagger-bearer," should not be thought of as a sacrifice in the Hebrew sense of the word.

It is important to distinguish the different aspects under which the various offerings made to the gods, whether consisting of slain animals or of vegetable and liquid offerings, might be regarded.

i) They might be considered simply as the food of the gods. The gods had to be fed, and it was the duty of their worshipers to provide them with what was necessary for this purpose.

ii) Since, as we have seen, the god was regarded as the owner of the land, and those who cultivated it were his tenants, the offerings which they brought, whether livestock or the produce of the fields, were regarded as rent, dues paid to the divine lord of the land and city.

iii) It was regarded as necessary to keep the gods in good temper and to avert the consequences of their anger. This was called "appeasing the liver" of the gods, and offerings of butter, fat, honey, sweetmeats, as well as the choicest parts of the victims, were thought of as having this desirable effect.

iv) One important aspect of the slain victim is found in a number of ritual texts. This is its use as a *puhu*, or "substitute" for the person by whom it is employed. There are three different ways in which this principle of substitution was used in Babylonian and Assyrian ritual. First, the animal which served as a substitute for a sick person, since all sickness was regarded as the result of the anger of the gods or the hostility of evil demons, was sent away alive into a desert place, like the Hebrew scapegoat, carrying the sins or defilement of the person for whom it was the substitute. Second, the substitute animal, usually a kid, was regarded as the symbol of

Tammuz, and by the act of slaying the victim the sick man was thought of as being identified with the god in his death and subsequent resurrection, and thus delivered from the consequences of whatever he had done to cause his sickness. Thirdly, at certain grave crises in the history of the kingship, a human substitute might take the place of the king, and possibly even undergo death to avert evil consequences to the state. The connection of this substitution with the New Year ritual will be dealt with later. It would seem that the rite of human sacrifice as practiced in Canaan and in early Hebrew religion formed no part of the cultus in Babylonia and Assyria.

v) One final aspect of the offering may be mentioned. On the fifth day of the New Year Festival, a *mashmashu*, or exorcist-priest, together with a slaughtering priest, cut off the head of a sheep and with its carcass smeared the walls and door of the shrine, thus ceremonially wiping off any defilement on to the carcass of the sheep; then the head and carcass of the sheep were thrown into the river which carried them away together with the defilement they bore. The two priests who had carried out the purification, since they had become ritually unclean, were obliged to leave the city until the festival was over.

It will be seen that these various aspects of the offering did not include any exact parallel to the Hebrew burnt offering which was wholly consumed upon the altar before Yahweh "to make atonement" for the offerer. Nevertheless, the ritual of the scapegoat shows clear resemblances to the Babylonian *puhu*-ritual, and may well have been borrowed from it.

From the daily round of service to the gods we now turn to the central religious occasion of the Babylonian year. It is hardly necessary to emphasize the fact that the dwellers in the Tigris-Euphrates Valley were an agricultural people, hence the pattern of their religious year followed the procession of the seasons. The two high points in the farmer's year are the spring when the new growth appears, and the autumn when all the fruits of the earth have been safely gathered in. Either of these points may be regarded as the beginning of the year, and we know from the evidence of Babylonian ritual texts that both these seasons were the occasion of a New Year festival; at Erech and Ur, for instance, there was a spring and an autumn celebration. But at Babylon the festival was held during the first eleven days of Nisan, in the spring, and the importance of Babylon led to the general observance of the festival in the spring. The ritual texts which give us an account of what was done during the festival are not complete, but they cover the most important part of the proceedings. It would take too long to enumerate all the details of this full and elaborate performance, and we must be content to describe the most significant acts of the ritual.[1]

During the course of the festival the Epic of Creation (see p. 6off.) was recited twice, and it is probable that the series of ritual acts carried out were intended to be a dramatic re-enactment, with magical intent, of the main features of the Creation myth which the Epic embodies. These comprise a contest between Marduk and the Chaos Dragon, Tiamat, in which Marduk is victorious; at some point in the myth, not indicated in the Epic of Creation, but known to us from other sources, the god is vanquished and slain, and lies dead "in the mountain," probably represented by the ziqqurat, and is then restored to life by magical rites, in which the second chanting of the Epic has a part.

Connected in some way with the meaning of the myth at this point was a very significant piece of ritual in which the king played the principal part: on the fifth day the king was brought in by the priests and placed before the statue of Marduk where he was left alone. Then the high priest entered and removed from the king his royal insignia, which he laid on a stool before

[1] The full text of the Babylonian New Year ritual is given in the appendix.

the god; the priest then struck the king on the cheek, pulled his ears, and made him kneel before Marduk; in this position the king recited a set confession in which he declared his innocence of any acts which might injure Babylon; to this the priest replied by a blessing from the god and promises of success and prosperity. Thereupon the king rose and received his royal insignia again from the hands of the priest who again struck him smartly upon the cheek. The object of this strange procedure was to obtain an omen; if the blow produced tears the god was propitious, but if not Marduk was angry, and there would be disasters. This part of the ritual is evidently connected with the symbolic death and resurrection of the god enacted at this point in the New Year Festival, and has a double significance: on the one hand it reflects the agricultural purpose of the ritual, the use of magical means to promote the growth of the spring vegetation; on the other, it may point to an earlier period when the killing of the king and the institution of a younger and more virile successor was a seasonal event. (Some scholars doubt this.)

The remaining features of the ritual were a ceremony called "the fixing of destinies," determining the prosperity of the New Year; the very important ceremony of the Sacred Marriage, which probably took place in a chapel on the summit of the ziqqurat; in this ceremony the king represented the god, while a priestess of high rank played the part of the goddess. This piece of ritual was considered essential for the fertility of the land. Then there was a procession along the Sacred Way from Esagila to the *bit-akitu*, or Festival House outside the city; in this the king "took the hand" of Marduk, to lead the god out at the head of the procession, followed by all the visiting gods, the priests, and the populace. At some point in this period of the Festival there was a dramatic representation of the fight between Marduk and the Chaos Dragon, to which reference has already been made. It is possible that in Assyria this took the form of a contest between the king and a lion, or lions, procured for the purpose. Such is an outline of the greatest ritual occasion of the Babylonian and Assyrian year. In Assyria, the national god, Ashur, took the place of Marduk as the central figure of the ritual, but no Assyrian king was considered duly enthroned until he had "taken the hand" of Marduk at Babylon in the New Year Festival.

One other seasonal element of the cult may be mentioned, namely, that connected with the phases of the moon. The Babylonian religious calendar, while determined in part by the agricultural seasons, was originally a lunar calendar, like all early calendars, and the phases of the moon were carefully observed and were the subject of many omens. The two most important points of the moon's course, from the religious point of view, were the full moon (*shabattum*), and the day of the moon's total disappearance (*bubbulum*); the latter was regarded as a specially dangerous period, and was marked by fasting, prayers, and other rites. The new moon also was watched for, and its appearance, marking the beginning of the month, was an occasion for ritual. It is possible that the early Hebrew "new moons" and "sabbaths" (Isa. 1:13–14) were lunar festivals, marking new moon and full moon, and may go back to the common origin in ancient custom of both Babylonian and Canaanite lunar feasts. But it is extremely unlikely that the later Hebrew Sabbath, the seventh day of the week, had any connection with the Babylonian *shabattum*. In the Assyrian period the seventh, fourteenth, twenty-first, and twenty-eighth of the month were unlucky days, and the nineteenth was called "the day of wrath," and was marked by special fasts and prayers.

Before we leave the subject of seasonal feasts it may be remarked that it is probable that the various cities had their own seasonal calendars. For instance, the festal calendar of Lagash, going back to Sumerian times, is well known. There the New Year Festival was celebrated with the marriage of the goddess Bau to the god Ningirsu; there were also barley harvest, and malt festivals, and a festival at sheep shearing. Barley harvest and sheep shearing were also special religious occasions in early Hebrew religion.

We shall bring this part of our subject to an end with some description of a part of the cultus which played a large part in the daily life of the people. First, the belief in evil demons and their power was an ever-present preoccupation in the mind of the Babylonian. Every kind of sickness and misfortune was attributed to the malevolent activities of evil spirits, and the *ashipu*-priests were daily employed in performing rituals and reciting spells and incantations to ward off dangers or to cure diseases due to this cause. There were rituals and incantations for headache, toothache, fever, aphasia, spells for quieting a crying child, for reconciling estranged friends, for protecting women during pregnancy, a period when they were specially exposed to the attacks of a very malignant female demon named Lamashtu, whose horrific effigy has been preserved for us on a tablet intended to be hung up in the house, and containing an incantation against the Lamashtu. It is probable that this aspect of the cult occupied a much larger place in the mind and daily life of an ordinary Babylonian than the worship of the great gods.

Secondly, a department of the cult which employed the activities of a large class of priests and exercised a most important influence upon both public and private life was the observance, collection, and interpretation of omens. This was the special province of the *barû*-priests, or "seers," of whom something has already been said (see p. 54). Almost every kind of happening was regarded as having a religious significance, i.e., as indicating the disposition of the heavenly powers, whether favorable or unfavorable. Observation of the flight of birds, of the relation of the heavenly bodies to one another, of peculiar appearances in the sun or moon, of the appearance of the entrails and liver of sacrificed animals, of the position of arrows when thrown down on the ground, and many other phenomena, provided omens which were recorded and formed in the course of time an immense corpus of omen literature by the study of which the *barû*-priest was guided in interpreting the meaning of any particular omen. In the correspondence of the Assyrian kings we have many examples of the way in which decisions were sought from the priest on matters of state or on the conduct of a campaign. The king never went to war without a company of *barû*-priests in his train, and we read of Sennacherib's consulting his seers before beginning his various campaigns against Syria and Palestine. The collection of liver-omens goes back as far as the time of Sargon I, and the recent excavations at Mari have provided a collection of clay liver models which were used for the purpose of divination.

More will be said about the activities of the exorcist and diviner in Chapters VII and VIII, but this will give some idea of the general character of the cultus and of the extent to which it entered into the life of the people.

We shall now pass on to another very important element in the religion of Babylon and Assyria, namely, the mythology. A link of transition is furnished by the fact that the omen-texts, provide us with much valuable material for supplementing the actual mythological texts which have come down to us.

CHAPTER VI

BABYLONIAN AND ASSYRIAN MYTHOLOGY

N O ancient civilization and no early religion known to us is without a mythology. The myth is therefore an important element in the culture of any people, and nowhere has it a more significant place than in the religion of the Babylonians and Assyrians.

When we come to examine the myths which have been preserved in the extensive remains of Babylonian and Assyrian religious literature, we find that there are two main classes of myths; these may be called *ritual* myths and *origin* myths. It is not easy to say which of the two types of myth is the earlier, nor are they always easy to distinguish from one another. The best known Babylonian myth, for instance, the Creation myth, is clearly shown by its use in the New Year Festival to be a ritual myth, while it also appears to offer an explanation of how the ordered universe came into being, and partakes of the character of an origin myth. But anthropology seems to suggest that man's primal need, when confronted by a mysterious and often hostile environment, was not to explain its origin, but to evolve an effective pattern of action in order to secure the conditions of a good life. Hence there is a strong probability that the ritual myth, in which the myth is the spoken part of the ritual and has a magical potency of its own, was the earliest form of myth. But the dividing line is often hard to draw, and there are certain myths, of which the famous Epic of Gilgamesh is an example, which Professor Dhorme has called "heroic myths," and which are difficult to classify under either of the above main types. Hence, in this chapter we shall not attempt any hard and fast classification, but shall give an account of the most important Babylonian and Assyrian myths known to us.

But first it may be interesting to offer here, for purposes of comparison, another classification of myths, namely that of Professor Thorkild Jacobsen: "The questions which the prolific and varied mythological literature of the third millennium posed and answered may be summed up, for the greater part, under three heads. There are, first, *myths of origin* which ask about the origin of some particular entity within the cosmos or some group of such entities: gods, plants, men. The answer is usually given in terms of birth, more rarely in terms of creation or craftsmanship. The second group consists of *myths of organization*. The myths of this group ask how some feature within, or some area of, the existing world order was brought about: how some god or other obtained his function and offices, how agriculture became organized, how certain freak classes of human beings came to be and were assigned their status. The myths answer: 'By divine decree.' Lastly, in a sense a subgroup under the myths of organization, there are *myths of evaluation*. The myths of this group ask by what right something or other holds its position in the world order. Such myths will weigh the farmer against the shepherd or, in a different approach to the same question, grain against wool; they will inquire into the relative merits of the costly gold and the lowly, but more useful, copper; etc. The evaluations implicit in the existing order are affirmed and traced to divine decision."[1]

It is possible that Professor Jacobsen would include what we have called *ritual* myths under one or other of the above classes. But it is difficult to avoid the conclusion that some myths have come into existence as the spoken part of a ritual, and are inseparable from the ritual in the sense that they, that is, the spoken words of the myth, do something, have the magic power of the ritual. Hence it seems justifiable to call such myths ritual myths, even if, from another aspect, they may be classed as myths of origin.

[1] *Ancient Near Eastern Texts*, ed. J. B. Pritchard, 151–52.

The Creation Myth. We have already spoken about the late form of the myth of Creation as we meet it in the chant which was sung at an important point in the New Year Festival at Babylon. But behind this late recension of the myth there lie several older and divergent forms. In an early Sumerian version of the story of Creation the three great gods of the Sumerian pantheon, Anu, Enlil, and Enki (i.e., Ea), with the help of the goddess Ninkharsagga, co-operate in the work of creation; there is no struggle, such as we find in the Epic of Creation, and the creative activity of the gods is described as extended to the creation of the five Antediluvian cities; the account goes on to describe the Deluge, which is here directly connected with the work of creation. In the Epic of Creation the Deluge is not mentioned, and, as we shall see, the Babylonian myth of the Deluge has no connection with the creative activity of the gods, but has reached us as part of the Epic of Gilgamesh.

In another version the god Gilimma is represented as creating the earth by binding a bundle of reeds and pouring soil upon it, clearly a picture of the way in which the early Sumerian settlers made cultivated settlements possible in the marshes of the river valley. (This myth also enters into the ritual of the New Year Festival.)[2]

There is also a fragmentary text in which Ea and the goddess Aruru co-operate in the creation of man out of clay by magical incantations.

But all these earlier versions were superseded in Babylonia by the classic version contained in the *Enuma Elish*, the Babylonian name for the Epic of Creation, and this we will now describe.

The first part of the poem contains an account of what the universe was like before the events took place which resulted in the creation by Marduk of a new world order. It describes a time when there was no sky and no earth, but only a watery chaos composed of the mingled waters of Apsu, the abyss of

[2] *Myth and Ritual*, ed. S. H. Hooke, 54.

sweet waters, Tiamat, the salt water ocean, and Mummu, who may, as Professor Jacobsen suggests, represent cloud banks and mist; there were no marshes and no islands, and no gods had come into being. It is probable that the Hebrew description of a primeval watery chaos existing before the divine creative activity began derives from this source. Then follows a genealogy of the gods: the first pair, Lahmu and Lahamu produced Anshar and Kishar; the firstborn of Anshar was Anu, and Anu "begot in his image Nudimmud," i.e., Ea, who had no rival among the gods. The noisy and unruly behavior of these younger gods annoyed their parents Apsu and Tiamat, who, by the advice of Mummu, Apsu's vizier, planned to destroy the gods whom they had made. But Ea became aware of their plan and foiled it by his magical powers. He slew Apsu, bound Mummu and rendered him helpless; he then made Apsu, the Deep, his own sacred chamber, where his son Marduk was born. The poem goes on to describe the amazing physical characteristics and powers of the great son of Ea, fitting him for his future destiny.

Tiamat is then stirred up by her brood to a fresh attack upon Anu and his circle of younger heavenly gods. She confers magical powers upon her second husband, Kingu, and invests him with the Tablets of Destiny. She creates an army of monstrous dragon and serpent forms, armed with poison fangs, and places Kingu at their head. When the news reaches the assembly of the gods they are filled with dismay. First Ea and then Anu fail to cope with the situation; finally Anshar arises and proposes that Marduk be appointed as the champion of the gods and sent against Tiamat and her monsters. Marduk accepts the task on the condition that he be made first among the gods and that his word shall have the force of the decree of Anu. His condition is accepted; he is invested with the powers and insignia of kingship by the assembled gods, and his word is declared to have the authority of Anu; his possession of this power is proved before the company of the gods by his causing a mantle to disappear and then reappear magically. Marduk is then armed "with matchless weapons"; he makes a bow and fits an arrow to the cord; he grasps his mace; he arms himself with the lightning and fills his body with flame; he makes a net to take Tiamat, and stations the four winds to prevent her escape; he raises the seven stormwinds to follow him and mounts his storm chariot. When the two hostile forces meet, Marduk challenges Tiamat to single combat; as she opens her mouth to consume him he drives in his winds to distend her, pierces her belly with his arrow, slays her and tramples upon her carcass. He binds Kingu, takes from him the Tablets of Destiny and fastens them upon his own breast. He then splits the body of Tiamat into two parts, "like a shell-fish," and fixes half of it on high as sky to hold back the waters of the heavenly ocean. He then assigns to Anu, Enlil, and Ea their portions of the heavenly ecliptic. This part of the myth occupies the first four tablets of the Babylonian form of the epic.

Tablet V describes how, after his victory over the forces of chaos, Marduk proceeds to set the universe in order and arranges the calendar, especially ordering the phases of the moon. Unfortunately, only the first twenty-two lines of this tablet are sufficiently intact to be legible, and we cannot tell what led up to the creation of man, which is described in the first half of the sixth tablet. There are several interesting and important features in this account which call for notice. First, the purpose of man's creation is to set the gods free from menial tasks: Marduk is represented as saying in the assembly of the gods, "Man I will create. He shall be charged with the service of the gods that they may be at ease." Secondly, in order that the gods may be freed a substitute must be provided; there must be death in order that the new life may come into existence. The substitute is found in the guilty person of Kingu, who is convicted in the assembly of the gods of having incited the insurrection of Tiamat; accordingly Kingu is executed, and out of his blood, by the magic skill of Ea, man is created, and upon him the service of the gods is imposed.

Then Marduk, as king of the gods, divides the Anunnaki of

heaven and earth into two groups under the command of Anu; three hundred are to stand guard in heaven, and three hundred on earth. There follows the account of the building of Marduk's temple, Esagila, by the Anunnaki in gratitude for their deliverance, and a description of the great banquet which celebrated its completion. The last part of Tablet VI and the whole of Tablet VII are occupied with the proclamation by Anu, in the assembly of the gods, of the fifty names of Marduk.

The above summary of the contents of this great Babylonian liturgy, embodying the myth of creation as it was current in Babylon from about the middle of the second millennium B.C., is based upon the latest version of the text as translated by Professor E. A. Speiser and published in *Near Eastern Texts relating to the Old Testament* (ed. J. B. Pritchard, Princeton University Press, 1950). An admirable commentary on it by Professor Thorkild Jacobsen may be found in Chapter V of *The Intellectual Adventure of Ancient Man* (ed. H. Frankfort, University of Chicago Press, 1946). It should be remarked that in the Assyrian form of the myth the god Ashur replaces Marduk as the hero of the story.

The next great mythological text to be described is that generally known as the Epic of Gilgamesh. This also, like the Enuma Elish, has had a long literary history, and its Akkadian form, which rests upon Sumerian sources, may be assigned to the beginning of the second millennium B.C. The poem consists of twelve tablets, some of which are in a fragmentary condition; the best-preserved is the eleventh tablet containing the well-known Babylonian version of the Flood myth. Much fresh light has been thrown on the myth by recent researches, especially by the work of Professor Kramer and Mr. C. J. Gadd of the British Museum. Professor Kramer's results have been published in a volume entitled *Sumerian Mythology* (Memoirs of the American Philosophical Society, vol. xxi, 1944). The most recent translation is to be found in the collection of Near Eastern Texts mentioned above.

The poem is a heroic epic concerned with the exploits of Gilgamesh, a legendary king of Erech, whose name occurs in the Sumerian king-lists in the second dynasty after the Flood, as the successor to Dumuzi, i.e., Tammuz, the Fisherman. According to the myth, Gilgamesh was two-thirds god and one-third man, and was endowed by the gods with superhuman size and strength. The story begins by describing how the people of Erech complained to Anu of the arrogance of Gilgamesh and his tyranny over the city. In answer to their plaint the goddess Aruru, who had made Gilgamesh, creates a wild man, Enkidu, who is the equal of Gilgamesh in strength; he lives on grass and is a companion of the wild beasts. When the news came to Gilgamesh of the existence of Enkidu and of how he was preventing the hunters from catching game, he ordered a temple prostitute to be sent to entrap Enkidu who had never known such pleasures. She went out to the forest and lay by one of the watering places, and displayed her charms to Enkidu when he came to drink with the wild beasts. He took her and had pleasure of her for seven days, but when he tried to join his animal companions again they fled from him. His seducer explained to him that he had undergone a change, "Thou art wise, Enkidu, thou art become like a god." He was no longer a meet companion for the gazelles, and the harlot told him of the might and glory of Gilgamesh, stirring him with the ambition to challenge Gilgamesh to a trial of strength.

At this point the first tablet ends. The second tablet describes the entry of Enkidu into Erech and his titanic wrestle with Gilgamesh, ending in a reconciliation and a pledging of friendship between them. The next three tablets give an account of the first of the joint adventures of Gilgamesh and Enkidu. In spite of Enkidu's attempts to dissuade him, Gilgamesh determines to invade the Cedar Forest and attack its terrible guardian, the fire-breathing giant Huwawa (in the Assyrian version the name is written in the more familiar form Humbaba). In spite of many gaps in the various sources, enough of the text is intelligible to

Marduk, chief god of Babylon, on piece of lapis. About 1500
B.C. Staatliche Museum, Berlin.

Assyrian deity plucking fruit from the sacred tree. Metropolitan Museum of Art, New York.

make it clear that with the help of Shamash and of the goddess Ninsun, the mother of Gilgamesh, the adventure was successful and ended with the slaying of Huwawa.

Tablets VI to VIII deal with the events which lead to the death of Enkidu. First we have an account of how Ishtar invites Gilgamesh to be her lover, and how the hero contemptuously rejects her approaches, reminding her of the wretched fate of all her former lovers. Ishtar, mad with rage, demands of Anu that he shall create the Bull of heaven for the destruction of Gilgamesh, and threatens, if he refuses, to break open the doors of the nether world and let loose all the dead upon the earth. So the Bull is created and begins to wreak havoc upon earth, but it is quickly vanquished and slain by Gilgamesh and Enkidu. Such flouting of the heavenly powers cannot be permitted, and in the assembly of the gods Enlil demands the death of Enkidu in punishment for this arrogance. Enkidu dies, and the close of Table VI describes the lamentation of Gilgamesh over his friend. It may also be noted here that lines thirty-three to thirty-nine of Tablet VII contain the famous description of the state of the dead in the Babylonian underworld—"He leads me (Enkidu) to the House of Darkness, the abode of Irkalla, to the house which none leave who have entered it, on the road from which there is no way back, to the house wherein the dwellers are bereft of light, where dust is their fare and clay their food. They are clothed like birds, with wings for garments, and see no light, residing in darkness."

The death of Enkidu causes Gilgamesh to set out on the quest for some way of escaping his friend's fate and avoiding the terrible doom of death. According to ancient tradition the only mortal who had been granted the gift of immortality by the gods was his ancestor Utnapishtim, the sole survivor of the Flood. Gilgamesh now determines to find Utnapishtim and learn from him the secret of immortality. Tablets IX to XI contain the account of the adventures which befell Gilgamesh on his perilous journey in search of Utnapishtim. First he comes to the mountain range of Mashu, guarded by the scorpion-man and his wife, and which no mortal had ever crossed. The guardians allow him to pass; he follows "the way of the sun," and after twelve leagues of darkness arrives at an earthly paradise the description of which is lost by the mutilation of the last column of the tablet. At the beginning of Tablet X Gilgamesh is found in conversation with the ale-wife Siduri, who seems to be a form of Ishtar. She tries to dissuade him from the next stage of his journey, which is the crossing of the Waters of Death. His quest is vain, she says, for "The life thou pursuest thou shalt not find. When the gods created mankind, death for mankind they set aside, life in their own hands retaining." However, seeing he will not be turned aside from his purpose, she advises him to consult Urshanabi, the boatman of Utnapishtim, by whose help he may be able to cross the Waters of Death.

Gilgamesh finds Urshanabi, who tells him to go into the forest and cut down 120 poles; this done, they launch the boat and reach the Waters of Death after a run of a month and a half. Then Urshanabi tells Gilgamesh to push the boat by the poles, dropping them one by one, and not letting his hands touch the Waters of Death. Thus Gilgamesh arrives at last at "the mouth of the rivers," the place which the gods had assigned to Utnapishtim and his wife for their eternal dwelling; he lays before his ancestor the object of his quest and asks how he had acquired the gift of immortality. In answer, Utnapishtim relates to him the story of the Flood, and it should be noted here that the Assyrian version which has become the standard form of the myth differs in many details from what we know of the earlier Sumerian version which is connected with the Creation myth. Utnapishtim tells Gilgamesh that when he dwelt in the ancient city of Shurippak the gods decided to destroy mankind by a flood. The plan was supposed to be secret, but Ea, being friendly to mankind, revealed the secret by repeating the words of the gods to the reed hut, which passed them on to Utnapishtim. Acting on Ea's instructions Utnapishtim built a ship of strange shape and dimensions, for it would seem to have been a perfect cube; it had six decks, and its floor plan was divided into nine parts; but it is possible that the measurements relate to the hold of the ship. Some scholars have held that in shape the ship was like a giant *kuffah*, or circular boat such as has been used for transport on the Euphrates from time immemorial. Utnapishtim gathered into the ship his possessions, his family, and all kinds of cattle and wild beasts. The Flood lasted seven days, till "all of mankind had returned to clay." The ship grounded on Mt. Nisir, and after waiting seven days Utnapishtim sent out in succession a dove, a swallow, and a raven. When the raven did not return Utnapishtim opened the ship and let out all its living freight; he then offered sacrifices, and we are told that the gods smelled the savor of the sacrifices and gathered like flies about the sacrificer.

Then follows a description of the scene in the assembly of the gods, where Ishtar laments the destruction of her people, and blames Enlil for the Flood; she swears by her necklace of lapis never to forget the days of the Flood. Enlil is enraged at the escape of some of mankind, and accuses Ea of having betrayed the secret of the gods. Ea appeases Enlil, and Enlil then declares that Utnapishtim and his wife shall be like the gods and live for ever at the mouth of the rivers. Here ends Utnapishtim's story of the Flood; he then goes on to tell Gilgamesh that his quest is hopeless, and shows him that he cannot even contend with sleep, how much less with death. The cirumstances under which Utnapishtim had been granted immortality are unique and cannot be repeated. As some compensation for his disappointment Utnapishtim then tells Gilgamesh of a magic herb which grows at the bottom of the sea and has the power of making the old young again. Gilgamesh dives and brings up the plant and sets off on his return to Erech, intending to use the magical properties of the plant for the benefit of himself and his people. On the way back Gilgamesh finds a pool of fresh water and stops to bathe in it. While he is bathing a serpent comes up from the pool and carries off the plant; as it goes it sloughs its skin, while Gilgamesh is left to lament his loss. Here the eleventh tablet ends.

The twelfth tablet forms no part of the epic proper, although it belongs to the Sumerian cycle of the traditions about the hero, and has been shown by Mr. Gadd to be a direct translation from a Sumerian original. It deals with two magical objects, the *pukku* and the *mikku*, possibly a magic drum and drumstick, which Inanna had given to Gilgamesh and which had fallen into the underworld. Gilgamesh laments their loss, and Enkidu offers to go down into the underworld to recover them. Gilgamesh warns him that if he is to succeed he must observe certain taboos, apparently belonging to ancient funerary ritual. Enkidu fails to observe the taboos and is unable to return from the nether world. Gilgamesh tries in vain to get Enlil and Sin to intercede with the gods of the lower world, but finally gets Ea to intercede with Nergal who opens a hole in the ground from which the spirit of Enkidu issues forth like a puff of wind. Enkidu gives Gilgamesh information about the state of the dead in the under-world and there the tablet breaks off. It is clear that other fragments of the Gilgamesh saga exist. Some of these have already been published, and one, published by Professor Albright in BASOR 94, contains an account of the death of Gilgamesh. But it is also clear from the scattered Sumerian traditions, oral or written, that some Babylonian author has composed a great epic poem with Gilgamesh as its hero, whose underlying theme is the sadness and frustration of human mortality. There is reason to suppose that some of the Sumerian sources may represent ritual myths, and the last tablet, as Mr. Gadd has suggested, points to a connection with funerary ritual. The connection between the Hebrew Flood stories and the myth contained in the Gilgamesh Epic has long been observed and few today would deny that the Hebrew forms of the story, for there are at least two, must be indebted to some ancient Sumerian or Babylonian source.

Another early Babylonian and Assyrian myth, whose theme

is also the loss of immortality, is that which goes by the name of the Myth of Adapa. It was widely known, for the oldest and fullest form of the myth was found among the Tell el-Amarna Tablets, and seems to have been used by Egyptian scribes as a text for learning cuneiform.

According to the myth, Adapa, whose name has been equated by Ebeling with Adam, was created by Ea as "the model of men," hence presumably the first man. He was king and priest of Eridu, the most ancient of the Sumerian cities. When he was fishing in the Persian Gulf the south wind overturned his boat, so he broke the wing of the south wind. For seven days the south wind did not blow, and Anu inquired the reason for this; when he was told what Adapa had done he ordered him to appear before him. Ea then instructed his son how to conduct himself; he was to put on mourning attire, and when he came to the guardian deities of the heavenly gate, Tammuz and Ningizzida, he was to explain to them that he was in mourning for their disappearance from the earth, so obtaining their favor and gaining admittance. Ea further told him that when he came before the gods he would be offered bread of death and water of death which he must refuse, but he might put on the garment and anoint himself with the oil which they would offer him.

He obediently followed these instructions, was favorably received by Tammuz and Ningizzida, and when Anu asked why he had broken the wing of the south wind he explained the circumstances. Anu was appeased and ordered bread of life and water of life to be offered to Adapa; but he, obedient to his father's instructions, refused them. Then Anu laughed at him and told him that he had refused the gift of immortality; henceforward disease and death must be the lot of mankind. So both these ancient myths deal with the troubling question of why men die, but behind the myth of Adapa there lies the feeling that it was by some trick or jealousy of the gods, in this instance of Ea, that mankind had been deprived of the gift of eternal life.

Many other myths and fragments of myths have survived

from Sumerian times, coming down to us through Babylonian and Assyrian versions, and some even from Hittite translations, but it is not possible to give them all here. Some deal with the problem of kingship and its origin; of these the most important are the myth of Etana and the myth of Zu. Etana is found in the Sumerian king-list among the kings of the first dynasty after the Flood. The myth is intended to explain how kingship came down from heaven, and Etana was designated by the gods as the first king. But he had no child to secure the succession, and the myth relates how it was necessary for Etana to ascend to heaven in order to bring down the plant of birth. Etana enlisted the help of the eagle whom he had previously delivered from a desperate situation, and the eagle carries him up on its back to the heaven of Anu where he would seem to have obtained that which he came to seek, since in the king-list his son is named as succeeding him. The myth gives a remarkable description of how, as Etana and the eagle ascend league upon league, the land shrinks until it appears like a gardener's ditch. There is a well-known Babylonian seal depicting the beginning of Etana's flight. (See Frankfort, *Cylinder Seals*, Pl. xxiv h.)

The myth of Zu, the bird-god, deals with another aspect of the same theme of kingship, this time the kingship in heaven. According to the conception preserved in this myth, the *Elli-lutu*, the Enlilship, or sovereignty in heaven, depended on the possession of the Tablets of Destiny, whose significance we have already seen in the Epic of Creation. In the myth of Zu these emblems of kingship have been stolen by the bird-god Zu, and the heavenly gods are dismayed. Anu orders Adad to go against Zu, but he declines the adventure, so does a second, but a third whose name is not evident owing to the fragmentary state of the texts apparently succeeds in bringing Zu to judgment and recovering the Tablets of Destiny. An early Sumerian fragment suggests that Lugalbanda did it, while a Babylonian hymn of the time of Ashurbanipal assigns the honor of crushing the skull of Zu to Marduk. The theme appears on several Babylonian seals. (See *Cylinder Seals*, Pl. xxiii, e and f.)

Several myths deal with the subject of the underworld, its rulers and their relations with the heavenly gods. There is the myth of Nergal and Ereshkigal which tells how Nergal became the ruler of the nether world. There is the striking *Vision of the Nether World* known to us in von Soden's excellent translation given in an English version in *Ancient Near Eastern Texts*. But the longest and most important is the myth of the Descent of Ishtar to the Nether World whose Akkadian form is based on the Sumerian myth of Inanna's descent into the underworld but differs from the Sumerian version in various details. The Akkadian text describes the descent of Ishtar into the underworld, but gives no explanation for her action. We have the well-known account of Ishtar being stripped of successive articles of adornment and apparel as she passes through each of the seven gates. She is locked up by Ereshkigal, and during her absence in the underworld all fertility of procreation ceases on earth. There is distress in heaven, but Ea creates a eunuch and sends him down to the underworld to trick Ereshkigal into releasing Ishtar. His plan succeeds and Ishtar is released and returns to the upper world. The text concludes with a passage which introduces Tammuz as welcoming Ishtar on her return; it runs as follows: "On the day when Tammuz welcomes me, when with him the lapis flute and the carnelian ring welcome me, when with him the wailing men and the wailing women welcome me, may the dead rise and smell the incense." The Sumerian form of the myth contains no reference to the death of Tammuz and his descent into the underworld, which in various Tammuz liturgies is represented as the motive for Ishtar's descent. Hence the reference here is unexpected and difficult to explain.

We shall bring this chapter to a close with a translation of the myth of the Worm and the Tooth. It is a good example of the intimate connection between myth and ritual, and is found

in an incantation text which goes back to the Old Babylonian
period:

> After Anu had created heaven,
> Heaven had created the earth,
> The earth had created the canals,
> The canals had created the marsh,
> And the marsh had created the worm—
> The worm went, weeping, before Shamash,
> His tears flowing before Ea:
> "What will thou give me for my food?
> What wilt thou give me for my sucking?"
> "I shall give thee the ripe fig,
> And the apricot."
> "Of what use are they to me, the ripe fig
> And the apricot?
> Lift me up and among the teeth
> And the gums cause me to dwell.
> The blood of the tooth I will suck,
> And of the gum I will gnaw
> Its roots."
>> Fix the pin and seize its foot. (This is an instruction
>>> to the dentist who would, of course, be a priest.)
> "Because thou hast said this, O worm,
> May Ea smite thee with the might
> Of his hand!"

(There follow details about the treatment, the injunction to
recite this incantation three times, the remark that the text had
been copied from an ancient tablet, and the name of the scribe.)
From *Ancient Near Eastern Texts*, p. 100.

CHAPTER VII

RELIGION AND DAILY LIFE

A visitor from another planet, looking down upon the dome of St. Paul's dominating the city from its eminence, and seeing too the thousands of church spires around it, might well infer that London was wholly devoted to religious observances, an ill-founded inference, as we know too well. But the Mesopotamian migrant, passing from city to city in the Euphrates Plain and seeing in each city the towering ziqqurat surrounded by its complex of temple buildings, with its swarm of priests hurrying to and fro about their daily business, would have been fully justified in supposing that Babylonian life was permeated by religious activities.

What we have already seen in the rituals and myths of Babylon and Assyria has shown that from birth to death the life of the Babylonian or Assyrian citizen was enfolded and directed by religious conceptions and practices. It is obvious that the great festivals would affect the lives of ordinary individuals as occasion of public rejoicing and feasting, but it is necessary, in order to make the picture of Babylonian and Assyrian religion complete, to give some account of how the religion affected the more intimate aspects of daily life.

An eminent Assyriologist has said, "The *ashipu*-priest, i.e., the exorcist, is the father confessor of the Assyro-Babylonian community."[1] We have already, in Chapter IV, given some account of the functions of the *ashipu*, *mashmashu*, and *barû* priests, but further details must now be added, since these were the priests whose activities were most in demand by ordinary members of the community. One of the most important factors in the daily life of a Babylonian was the fear of devils and evil spirits, and to a lesser degree the fear of offended gods. In the

[1] Ebeling, *Aus dem Tagewerk*, 3.

ritual texts, such as the collections of incantations called *Maqlu* and *Shurpu*, and in many of the mythological texts, we find many of the demons mentioned by name. Most of the names are Sumerian, though some are Semitic, and it is probable that the Semitic settlers adopted the Sumerian demonology together with the general pattern of their culture and religion. Specially feared were the spirits of the dead who had not had the due burial rites performed over them, or had died under ill-omened circumstances. Many of the demons were supposed to be the offspring of Anu and Enlil, the two of the triad of high gods who were on the whole unfriendly to men, while many more were the offspring of the underworld gods. On the other hand the third of the great triad, Ea, was always friendly to men, and was regarded as the source of the protective arts of magic and incantation upon which mortals depended for defense against the assaults of all the hostile supernatural powers. Hence, also, Ea was the patron god of the various orders of priests who had been trained in the practice of exorcism, in the knowledge of spells and incantations, and in the interpretation of dreams and omens. These were the people to whom the Babylonian turned for help in any kind of trouble or perplexity.

In this connection it must also be remarked that there were people who possessed the same kind of knowledge but used it to do harm to their fellow men; these were the sorcerers and witches whose baleful activities are reflected in the various prayers and spells preserved in such collections as *Maqlu* and *Shurpu* already mentioned. As early as the time of Gudea of Lagash, about the middle of the third millennium B.C., we find legislation against this antisocial class of persons, evidently unsuccessful. About the middle of the second millennium B.C., in the Middle Assyrian Laws (ed. G. R. Driver and J. C. Miles, 1935), we have a section dealing with the practice of witchcraft; it runs as follows: "If either a man or a woman have made magical preparations and they have been seized in their hands and charge and proof have been brought against them, the maker of the magical preparations shall be put to death. The man who saw the making of the magical preparations and heard from the mouth of an eyewitness of the magical preparations who told him saying, 'I myself saw it,' shall come forward as an earwitness and tell the king; if what he has told is denied by the eyewitness, he shall make a statement in the presence of the Bull the Son of the Sungod saying: 'On my oath, he said it'; and then he is quit. As for the eyewitness who told it and denied it—the king shall interrogate him in such a way as he thinks fit and shall read his inmost thoughts. The exorcist when he is fetched shall make the man speak, and the former (i.e., the exorcist) shall speak, saying: 'From the adjuration wherewith thou hast been adjured before the king and his son, they will not release thee; thou hast surely been adjured according to the words of the tablet wherewith thou hast been adjured before the king and his son.' "[2] Here it is to be noted that in Assyria the penalty for practicing sorcery (*kishpu*) is death, as it is also in the Hebrew codes. Also it is interesting to see that, in the case of a contumacious witness, the *ashipu* or exorcist is called in to adjure the witness by a particularly binding oath. The second clause of the Code of Hammurabi provides that a man who is charged with sorcery may submit himself to the ordeal of the river; if he drowned he was guilty and his accuser might take his property, but if he came out safe his accuser was put to death.

In the collection *maqlu*, already mentioned, the person who is reciting the incantation describes the witch as "she in whose heart the word of my misfortune dwells, on whose tongue my ruin is begotten, on whose lips my poison originates, in whose footsteps death stands." Since all kinds of disease or misfortune were attributed to the activities of evil spirits set in motion often by sorcerers or witches, it is not surprising that the magical texts are full of references to the *ashipu* and the part which he

[2] *Op. cit.*, 415–17.

played in the ceremonies which were intended to protect or deliver the Babylonian from the anger of the gods or the assaults of demons and evil spirits.

In the collection of texts which Ebeling has published under the title *Aus dem Tagewerk eines assyrischen Zauberpriesters*, we find the *ashipu* called in to perform rites for the protection of a pregnant woman (see p. 46), to quiet a crying child, to enable a man to reconcile an offended neighbor, to effect the confusion of an enemy, to insure favor for a suppliant before the king, or success in litigation. Many texts describe the activity of the *ashipu* in the performance of rituals to effect the cure of various diseases. Such ills as headaches, fevers, dumbness, nightmares, were attributed to the attacks of demons or the spirits of the dead, and the *ashipu* was called in to perform the rituals and recite the incantations proper to the particular case. The following is a typical example of what the *ashipu* was directed to do in the case of a man who had been seized by an *etimmu*, i.e., a ghost:

"When an *etimmu* has seized a man, (and) his heart cries out, you should sanctify yourself on a lucky day, (and) wash yourself with water from the cistern. You should go into the desert (and) sweep the ground with a palm twig. You should make an image in clay of the sick man as a substitute; you should clothe it with everyday clothes; you should set out twice seven loaves for his food, a spindle, a curtain, a nail, bind together to his (its) head. You should place an altar before Shamash; dates (and) fine meal you should sprinkle thereon, and place a censer with cypress perfume before it; you should place a small incense pot on it, (and) place that image before Shamash.

"Thus you should speak: *Incantation*, Father Ea, shining one, Father Ea who dost give effect to the incantation of Marduk, Eridu's son. Marduk has seen him . . . controller of heaven and earth, he who has given birth to all things, has sprinkled the sick man. End of the incantation.

"This incantation you should recite three times. You should

cut the cord of his clothing, (and) give him for food a cake baked in the ashes and two bowls of brewer's malt. You should take that image and bind it with a tamarisk twig, recite an incantation over it, (and) place it in position."

Then follows another long incantation, invoking the gods of the underworld, in whose power the sick man, represented by the clay image, is supposed to be. The closing lines of the tablet run, "Thou art buried, thou mayest change thyself, thou mayest change thyself (i.e., come to life again). *Incantation.* When a man is sick in the middle of his skull and his forehead."[3]

The general idea of the *ashipu's* actions, as in many other similar tablets, was based first of all on the principle of the *puhu*, or substitute. Such a substitute might be an animal, most frequently a kid, or, as in the example given above, a clay image; sometimes it might be an inanimate object, such as a staff. Whatever the form of the substitute, it was treated as dead and in the underworld. The ritual is often said to take place in the "desert," that being a common symbol of the underworld. Offerings are made to the gods of the underworld, funerary ritual is carried out, the incantation invokes Shamash, or Ea, or Marduk, life-giving gods, and the sick man is regarded as risen from the dead and thus freed from the malevolent grasp of the hostile power that had seized him, whether god, demon, or ghost.

It has been pointed out above that a large number of evil spirits and demons have names. Many of the names are those of diseases, others are names of hostile forces in nature, or of the characteristic activities of certain demons, e.g., we often hear of *Rabisu*, "the croucher," because he was supposed to lie in wait secretly. An obscure verse in Gen. 4:7 has been explained, no doubt correctly, as an allusion to this crouching demon. The reason why the demons and evil spirits were given names was that the ancient Semites, and no doubt the Sumerians also, believed in the magic potency of names. In order to be in a position to get control over a demon, or over a person, it was

---

[3] Meissner, *Babylonien und Assyrien*, II, 235–36.

necessary to know his name and use it in a conjuration or spell.

Reference may be made here to a very common practice constantly found in exorcism tablets, viz., that of tying magic knots. The case was described earlier (see p. 46) of the use of magic knots tied by the *ashipu* for the protection of a pregnant woman. A magic knot could be tied by a sorcerer or witch to gain power over an enemy. By the loosing of the knot the power of the witch or sorcerer was broken. One of the *maqlu* tablets, directed against witchcraft, ends with the words, "Her knot is loosed, her sorcery is brought to nought, and all her charms fill the desert," where the desert symbolizes the underworld, as already pointed out above.

But sickness and sorcery were not the only occasions which called for the help of the *ashipu*. Supernatural dangers threatened most human activities. The building of a house could not be undertaken without due precautions. The most dangerous times in the course of the erection of a house were the laying of its foundations, and its completion. All public or sacred buildings had their foundation deposits, the placing of which was, no doubt, in earlier times accompanied by sacrifices. In Canaan these were frequently of children, as archeology has abundantly shown. Under the doors of private houses were buried amulets and figurines of gods, demons, or animals, to protect the dwellers in the house from evil spirits, and the presence of the *ashipu* would be required to pronounce the proper incantation. When the building was completed, the *ashipu* would come and place a clay figurine of the brick-god with provisions on a little boat to carry him away; he would then recite the incantation, "Brick-god, you are torn out, you are cut off, you are humbled. Brick-god, be adjured by heaven, be adjured by earth, be adjured by Alala and Belili, be adjured by Lahmu and Lahamu, be adjured by the gods who dwell in heaven, be adjured by the gods who dwell on earth, be adjured by Apsu (the Deep), be adjured by the gods who dwell in Duku (the shining mountain); may you be torn out, depart, be removed, be weakened, be gone from hence; I adjure you not to return."[4] The tablet goes on to direct that the *ashipu* and the builder should avert their faces, and throw seven tablets (?) to the right and seven tablets (?) to the left into the river. For three days the builder should not enter the house.

The great number of magical texts shows how intimately bound up with the daily life of the Babylonian or Assyrian was the art of the exorcist. The publican whose business was declining, the courtesan whose attractions were waning, the farmer who wanted more rain, or who wished to avert a plague of locusts, the courtier who wished to obtain favor at court, all such varied types of need are represented in the magical texts which provide the appropriate ritual and incantation for every situation. When we come to deal with the question of sin and atonement in Babylonian religion, we shall find that other aspects of the *ashipu's* activities will have to be considered, but we must turn now to the functions of the *barû*-priest and the way in which they affected the daily life of the Babylonian.

It was the special business of the *barû* to give the layman information about the shape of the future. The Babylonians and Assyrians believed that the future could be both controlled and predicted; they thought that everything which happened in the universe formed part of an intricate pattern of cause and effect, and that the meaning of the pattern could be ascertained by observing the course of events, even the most trivial. A most important part of the *barû's* activity consisted in the observation of the movements of the heavenly bodies, since the Babylonian believed that the course of events on earth, reflected and was determined by the course of events in heaven.

It may be relevant here to quote a significant passage from Professor Thorkild Jacobsen's discussion of the Mesopotamian idea of the cosmos as a state: "But human society was to the Mesopotamian merely a part of the larger society of the universe. The Mesopotamian universe—because it did not consist of

[4] Ebeling, *Tod and Leben*, 76–78.

dead matter, because every stone, every tree, every conceivable thing in it was a being with a will and character of its own—was likewise founded on authority; its members, too, willingly and automatically obeyed orders which made them act as they should act. These orders *we* call the laws of nature."[5] In the last resort, it was the will of the gods which shaped the course of events; but the will of the gods was not immutable, and the gods did not always will the same thing. Hence, on the one hand, it was thought possible, by prayers, penitence, and suitable offerings, to change the will of the gods, and in this sense the future could be controlled. On the other hand, by observing the sequence of events it was thought possible to establish a certain regularity in their connection which would enable the future to be predicted.

The result of many centuries of such observations is to be seen in the vast collection of omen-texts which has accrued from the excavation of many Mesopotamian sites. In addition to our knowledge of the omen-texts themselves, much light has been thrown on the activities of the *barû*-priests from the official letters of the Assyrian kings preserved in the library of Ashurbanipal at Nineveh. In one letter, for instance (Harper 223), we find the *barû* Nabu-zer-lishteshir writing to the king, "I have taken note of the portents, whether they came from the sky, from the earth, or from the underworld (?), as many as there were. I had them recited in order before Shamash." The writer of the letter goes on to promise the king success in quelling a rebellion. Another example of the interpretation of the omens comes from the same collection (Harper 1214), "In the month of Tammuz, on the night of the tenth, the constellation of the Scorpion draws near to the moon. This is the interpretation thereof: 'If, when the moon appears, the Scorpion stands by its right horn, locusts will go forth during the year and eat up the grain of the harvest. As for the king of Elam, he will be killed in that year, his reign will come to an end, an enemy will go

[5] Frankfort, *op. cit.*, 139.

forth and plunder his land. To the king of Akkad (will belong) an exalted sceptre, his reign will be long. If an enemy cross him, the overthrow of that enemy will be accomplished.' " As these and many other letters show, the *barû* had a close connection with the king and the court, and he was in constant consultation with the king concerning what the omens had to say about any proposed course of action; in time of war he was always at hand. We have a vivid picture in Hebrew literature of a consultation of the court prophets by Ahab with regard to his proposed campaign against the Syrians, and of the ritual which they used in giving responses (I Kings 22); there is also another illuminating reference in Ezek. 21:22–23 to the Babylonian methods of divination, "For the king of Babylon stood at the parting of the way, at the head of the two ways, to use divination: he shook the arrows to and fro, he consulted the teraphim, he looked in the liver; in his right hand was the divination for Jerusalem." But the custom of consulting the *barû* was not confined to kings and courts. The ordinary citizen resorted to him for guidance on all matters involving a knowledge of the future. If a merchant intended to set off on a business journey, or if a man wished to begin building a house, or to arrange for the marriage of his daughter, his first care was to find out from the *barû* whether the day he had chosen was a lucky one. Babylonian and Assyrian kings, in their numerous building inscriptions, always took care to say that the foundation stone had been laid in a lucky month and on a lucky day. It can be seen that the part played by the seer or *barû* in Babylonian life was of the highest importance, and we must now give a fuller account of the many and varied operations and techniques which are comprised under the term divination.

CHAPTER VIII

DIVINATION AND ITS TECHNIQUE

THE tradition of the practice of divination goes back to a very remote antiquity. The Sumerian version of the myth of the Flood describes the hero of that story as practicing divination, and the *barūtu*, or guild of seers, believed that it was the legendary king of Sippar, Enmeduranki, who received from the gods the art of divination and handed it on to the priesthood. The sun-god, Shamash, was the special patron of the *barūtu*, but most of the high gods also play a part in the rituals of divination. As early as the time of Ur-nanshe, priest-king of Lagash (*circ.* 3000 B.C.), an inscription mentions a person who is the "chief diviner," where the Sumerian word for "diviner" is the equivalent of the Akkadian *barû*. About a century later inscriptions of the time of Urukagina mention an official named *apkallu*, the expert in divination. Other evidence shows the continued and increasing importance of divination down to the time of Hammurabi of Babylon, during whose reign the divinatory practices of Sumer and Akkad were codified, and we have already seen in the previous chapter that the Assyrian kings had frequent recourse to the activities of the *barû*.

There are three words which define three different aspects of that which the diviner sought to ascertain, viz., *bîru*, vison, *purussu*, decision, and *ittu*, sign. The last of these is also found in Hebrew literature in the form '*ōth*. The *barû* sought to ascertain the will of the gods by dreams and visions which he was called upon to interpret; he sought in various ways to give decisions in affairs of state, which of course were the decisions of the gods; and by observation of signs or omens, as we have already seen, he accumulated a stock of significant instances upon which his decisions or advice were based. We have now to describe the various methods employed by the *barû* or seer to accomplish these ends.

The methods employed by the *barû* fall into two main classes, although the dividing line between them is not always easy to draw; they may be defined as natural and mechanical respectively. Under the heading "natural" may be classed dreams and visions, births, movements of animals, and, most important of all, astronomical and atmospheric phenomena, to the latter of which we shall devote a separate chapter. Under the name "mechanical" we may include what is called lecanomancy, i.e., the observation of the shapes taken by oil poured on the surface of water; next comes the examination of the internal organs of slain animals or sacrificial victims, especially those of sheep. While the entrails were a fertile source of omens, the study of the liver, known as hepatoscopy, formed a most important branch of the *barû's* activities. Models of the liver have been found, showing the surface of the organ divided into areas whose appearance constituted the ground for predictions. Recent excavations at Mari have yielded a number of clay models of the liver with inscriptions relating to their use for the purpose of omens. Under the same head come the practice of divination by arrows, called belomancy, referred to by Ezekiel (see p. 81), and the very widespread custom of divining by casting the sacred lots, a familiar example of which is the Hebrew use of Urim and Thummim, generally agreed to be some form of divination by the sacred lots. These various sources of omens and information concerning the future must now be briefly described.

From the earliest times dreams and night visions were regarded as the most direct means by which the gods communicated their will to men. The Epic of Gilgamesh contains the record of a number of dreams which came to Gilgamesh or to Enkidu, and the former is represented as turning to his goddess-mother, who "knew all things," for their interpretation. Gudea

83

of Lagash received in a dream instructions for the building of a temple. The records and inscriptions of the later Assyrian kings contain numerous instances of significant dreams. An example may be quoted from a letter written to Ashurbanipal by Marduk-shum-usur, probably a court *barû*: "In a dream the god Ashur said to (Sennacherib) the grandfather of the king my lord, 'O sage! You, the king, lord of kings, are the offspring of the sage and of Adapa. You surpass in knowledge Apsu and all craftsmen. When (Esarhaddon) the father of the king my lord went to Egypt, he saw in the region of Harran a temple of cedarwood. Therein the god Sin was leaning on a staff, with two crowns on his head. The god Nusku was standing before him. The father of the king my lord entered. (The god) placed (a crown) upon his head, saying, "You will go to countries, therein you will conquer!" He departed and conquered Egypt. The remaining countries not yet subject to the gods Ashur and Sin, the king, lord of kings, will conquer.' "[1] But dreams were not merely received, they might also be induced by the appropriate means. A special chamber in the temple was set apart for this purpose, and there, by the process called incubation, a special priest of the *barû* class, called a *shabru*, would induce a dream for the benefit of the inquirer, to whom the dream would then be interpreted by the *barû*. The principles of interpretation were based upon tradition, the body of dream material transmitted from age to age, and also upon the particular significance attached to different elements in the dream, numbers, movements, position, such as right or left, and other features which had already a definite meaning in the tradition of divination.

Birth omens, whether human or animal births, occupy a large part of the omen-texts. Birth itself was for the Babylonian a magical process, surrounded by ritual and accounted for by various myths. But for the diviner any abnormal kind of birth had special significance, and had to be observed and recorded.

[1] Pritchard, *A.N.E.T.*, 450.

Multiple births were noteworthy; the occurrence of actual monstrosities was, perhaps, helped out by imagination or dreams. We have such an omen recorded as, "When a woman gives birth to a child with the head of a lion, there will be a mighty king over the land. When a woman gives birth to a child with no right ear, the days of the prince will come to an end. When a woman gives birth to a child with a serpent's head, that is an omen of the god Ningizzida who devours the land; an omen of Gilgamesh who oppresses the land; a king exercising world-rule will be over the land."[2] There is also a group of omen-texts, closely related to the above, which lists various appearances of the human face and figure with their significance as omens, e.g., "When a man has duck's feet, he will become mighty. (This means) that his feet are broad and full of earth."[3]

Next come the omens drawn from the movements of animals, especially of birds. The behavior of domestic animals was closely observed; the king's chariot horses were the source of various royal omens; many omens were drawn from the behavior of dogs, as might be expected. For example, "When a white dog pisses on anyone, poverty will overtake him; if a black dog does the same, sickness will seize that man; if a brown dog does the same, that man will be joyful."[4] The behavior and flight of eagles and other birds of prey had special significance, "When a hawk is hunting, and passes from the right side of the king to his left, the king will be victorious whither he is going."[5] Nor were the actions of reptiles unnoticed; the ways and habits of snakes were always uncanny, especially the snake's power of renewal by casting its skin. The movements of snakes in the month of Nisan are the subject of a group of omens, "When from the first to the thirtieth of Nisan a snake falls behind a man,

[2] Meissner, *op. cit.*, II, 264.

[3] Kraus, *Die physiognomischen Omina der Babylonier*, 63.

[4] Meissner, *op. cit.*, II, 260–61.

[5] *Id.*, *op. cit.*, II, 260.

his friend will be changed into his enemy."[6] Closely associated with this class of omens is the significance of right and left hand, as in the hawk omen above. In general the right hand was of good omen, but the left hand was the opposite because it looked towards hostile Elam; hence the widespread meaning of the word "sinister." The most important of the omens drawn from natural sources, namely, those based on the observation of astronomical and atmospheric phenomena will be dealt with in the next chapter, hence we shall turn now to the mechanical or artificial methods of obtaining omens.

The form of divination called lecanomancy consisted of dropping oil, or sometimes flour, upon the surface of water in a bowl. Omens were drawn from the shapes assumed by the floating oil or flour. In a tablet going back to the time of Hammurabi of Babylon we read, "When the oil forms a ring towards the east and remains (unbroken): for a journey—I will undertake it and eat a portion (i.e., take a share in the profit accruing from a business venture): for a sick person—he will get well. When the oil forms two circles, one large and one small, the man's wife will give birth to a boy; for a sick person—he will get well. When the oil spreads and fills a cup, the sick person will die: for a journey—it will cause the death of those taking part in it."[7] The divination of Joseph's cup, mentioned in Gen. 44:5, was probably of this kind.

Of the two methods of divining by the internal organs of a slain animal, viz., by the entrails and the liver, the latter was the most important and widespread, although the appearance of the entrails and the heart also had great value as a source of omens. Both these methods were carried far beyond Mesopotamia and were used by Etruscan and Roman haruspices. The famous bronze model of the liver discovered at Piacenza in 1877 is a witness to the diffusion of the Babylonian method of hepatoscopy. According to Semitic psychology the heart was the seat

[6] *Id., op. cit.,* II, 261.
[7] Meissner, *op. cit.,* II, 275.

of the intelligence, while the bowels and the liver were the seat of the emotions. The Babylonian ritual texts speak of appeasing the liver of the gods, and when Hosea says "Ephraim is a foolish dove without heart" (Hos. 7:11), he means that Ephraim is unable to understand the purposes of Israel's God.

The technical term used to designate the intestines as exposed for inspection was *irre sahiruti*, i.e., "entwined entrails." From the shape, color, and number of the entrails the *barû* drew his omens. Sometimes the entrails assumed the appearance of a grimacing face, which was called the face of Humbaba and has been preserved in effigy on clay tablets. Tradition takes this form of divination back to the time of Sargon I, as witness the following example: "When the entrails are completely inclosed by the gall bladder, this is an omen of Sargon who, on the strength of this oracle invaded Elam, subdued the Elamites, surrounded them and cut off their supplies."[8]

For the purposes of divination the liver was minutely mapped out, and the various divisions and protuberances were given names, such as "finger," "mouth," "palace," "standard," and so forth, and oracles based on the appearance of these different parts of the liver go back to the times of Sargon I and Naramsin. A very early clay model of the liver, divided into more than fifty compartments by vertical and horizontal lines, is dated as belonging to the first dynasty of Babylon. At the disposal of the priest who was learning the art of reading the liver were a number of manuals explaining the meaning of the different parts of the liver, and commenting on examples of the omens derived from them. The actual technique of observation was as follows: first the *barû* inspected the liver, gall, and the attached entrails as they lay in the opened stomach of the sheep; then with his left hand he lifted them up for closer examination; then the entrails were drawn out in order to expose completely the organs lying behind them. It then became possible to distinguish the favorable and unfavorable aspects of the liver itself.

[8] *Id., op. cit.*, II, 274.

In his manual the priest found such instructions as follows: "When the favorable signs are numerous and the unfavorable signs few, the oracle is favorable. But when the unfavorable signs are many and the favorable few, this oracle is unfavorable."[9] Again, "When the favorable and unfavorable signs are equally balanced, one should not depend on the luck of the oracle."[10] If a first inspection gave unfavorable results, a second and even a third might be undertaken in order to secure a favorable response. We have a record from the reign of Esarhaddon of an inquiry addressed to Shamash by the king concerning the suitability of the Scythian king Bartatua as a husband for his daughter. The inquiry was by means of the liver, and the record begins by entreating the god to overlook any imperfections in the victim or in the transmission of the god's message by the *barû*. The results of the first liver inspection, described in minute detail, were unfavorable; a second was immediately undertaken and gave favorable results, so that Esarhaddon was enabled to accept the Scythian king as a son-in-law.[11] The earlier liver-texts belonging to the time of the first Babylonian dynasty and the Cassite period, apparently consist of observations unaccompanied by interpretations, but, on the other hand, the texts from Ashurbanipal's library and the Neo-Babylonian temples were all provided with interpretations. They were also classified under the different divisions of the liver, in order to facilitate the inquirer's search. The pyramidal process of the liver was known in the omen-texts as the "finger"; here are some examples of the omens drawn from the appearance of the "finger": "When the 'finger' is like the head of a lion, his servants will expel the prince; when the 'finger' is like a lion's ear, the prince will have no rivals; when the 'finger' is like a sheep's head, the prince will be completely successful,"[12] and so forth.

[9] Meissner, *op. cit.*, II, 270.

[10] *Id., op. cit.*, II, 270–71.

[11] Meissner, *op. cit.*, II, 273.

[12] *Id., op. cit.*, II, 274.

Omens were also drawn from the kidneys; here comparison of the right and left gave significant omens, e.g., "When the right kidney is destroyed, the princess will die: for the weapons (i.e., in war), destruction of my lord; when the left kidney is destroyed, the princess of the hostile country will die: for the weapons, destruction of the hostile prince."[13] Examples might be multiplied indefinitely, but these will suffice to show the methods employed by the *barû* in divining by the internal organs of a slain animal. The principle, if any, underlying the whole method of divination seems to be purely empirical; sometimes coincidences repeated led to a particular interpretation; sometimes analogy or a mere play on words might lead to the formulation of an omen; but the religious element underneath what seems wholly mechanical lies in the belief that the entire complicated nexus of events was brought about by the will of the gods, so that the method of trial and error might well reveal to man's groping mind what that will was.

Divination by the casting of the lot, or by the shaking of the arrows, usually resorted to in answer to an inquiry, took the form of a response "yes" or "no," and the question was so framed as to call forth such a response. For example, in the case already referred to (see p. 81), when Ahab "inquired" of Yahweh about his proposed campaign against Syria, he put his question in a form which would call forth from the oracle a positive or a negative reply—"Shall I go up against Ramothgilead, or shall I forbear?" and received a positive answer, "Go up, for the Lord will deliver it into thy hand" (I Kings 22:6).

Before we turn to the most important branch of the diviner's activities, namely the observation of the movements of the heavenly bodies and of the weather, it may be remarked that among the numerous collections of omen-texts and manuals of divination there have been found collections of portents and prodigies which do not come under any of the above-mentioned heads, but which were considered to have ominous significance

[13] *Id., op. cit.,* II, 270.

and were therefore recorded. There is the famous collection of forty-seven portents which attended the downfall of Akkad; among these we find, "A severed head has cried aloud; a mare has a horn on the left side of her forehead; in Babylon a male date palm has borne dates; a lion, a hyena, and a wild boar have entered the city."[14] Some of the portents enumerated are incestuous crimes.

Moreover, in addition to the divinatory methods of ascertaining the will of the gods, there are recorded instances of prophetic utterances comparable to those of the Hebrew prophets. Those members of the *barūtu* who exercised this particular function were known as *mahhu*, a term which suggests something like the "ecstatic" condition usually attributed to certain phenomena of Hebrew prophecy. Several of the authors of such prophecies were women. The following is an example: "Fear not, Esarhaddon, I, the god Bel, speak to you. The beams of your heart I strengthen, like your mother who caused you to exist. Sixty great gods are standing together with me and protect you. The god Sin is at your right, the god Shamash at your left; sixty great gods stand round about you, ranged for battle. Do not trust men! Turn your eyes to me, look at me! I am Ishtar of Arbela; I have turned Ashur's favor unto you. When you were small, I sustained you. Fear not, praise me. Where is that enemy that blew over you when I did not notice? The future is like the past! I am the god Nabu, lord of the tablet stylus, praise me!

"Oracle from the lips of the woman Baia of Arbela."[15]

[14] Meissner, *op. cit.*, II, 277.
[15] Pritchard, *op. cit.*, 450.

CHAPTER IX

DIVINATION AND ASTROLOGY

IN a notable oracle of Deutero-Isaiah predicting the fall of Babylon, the poet apostrophizes the doomed city in the words, "Let now the astrologers, the star-gazers, the monthly prognosticators, stand up and save thee from the things that shall come upon thee" (Isa. 47:13). The Hebrew term for "astrologers" means "the dividers of the heavens," while the "monthly prognosticators" refers to an important function of the *barû*, namely, the determination of lucky and unlucky days and months. But by the time of Deutero-Isaiah Babylonian astrology was already very ancient, probably the oldest of all the methods of ascertaining the will of the gods. According to Babylonian belief the things which happened in heaven were the pattern of terrestrial events, and the movements of the celestial bodies determined human destinies. We have already seen (p. 62) how, in the ordering of the universe which followed the conquest of Tiamat, each of the great gods, Anu, Enlil, and Ea, was assigned his own portion of the heavens; within these "ways" of the gods, as they were called, the planets were assigned their stations. All the planets and stars, as then known to the Babylonians and Assyrians, had their names and were regarded as gods of greater or lesser degree, with their places in the mythology and the cult. Shamash, as the sun, and Adad, as the weather god, were the special patrons of the astrological aspect of divination, although many other divinities, such as Nannar, or Sin, the moon-god, and Ishtar, as Dilbat, or Venus, played an important part in the observations and calculations of the stargazers.

The earliest collection of celestial observations and their significance as omens is probably the ancient manual of astrology known by the title "When Anu and Enlil," which is believed to go back to the Sumerian period. Its antiquity is shown by its reference to the old fourfold division of the world into the lands of Akkad, Elam, Subartu, and Amurru, a division which is not found in later periods; also by the mention of such early kings as Rimush and Ibi-sin, going back to the middle of the third millennium B.C. Later on we find the Hittites and the Ahlamu mentioned, so that it is probable that the collection grew up through the centuries by the addition of the observations of succeeding generations of astrologers.

No doubt the ziqqurats would serve as observatories, but in the temples there was also a special chamber for the astrologers known as *bit tamarti*, "the house of observation," where they watched the moon; we find recorded, "On the twenty-ninth day we kept the watch in the house of observation: it was cloudy; we did not see the moon."[1] Naturally, this interest in the movements of the heavenly bodies gave rise to the calendar, and the accurate observations and calculations made by the Babylonian astrologers laid the foundation for the science of astronomy; but our concern is with the religious aspect of the subject, and the use to which the diviners put their knowledge of the heavens.

The moon was probably the first of the heavenly bodies to become the subject of observation. It is the nearest to the earth, and its changes are both regular and spectacular, so that its importance for the purposes of divination was recognized very early. Since the phases of the moon could not be determined with mathematical exactitude, the times of its disappearance and reappearance had to be watched with great care, and the variations in these had ominous significance. We have an early record relating to the ominous appearance of the moon in the intercalary month: "When, in this month, the moon is visible on the twenty-seventh day as on the first day of its appearance, it signifies misfortune for Elam; when the moon is visible on the twenty-eighth day as on the first day of its appearance, it betokens misfortune for Amurru";[2] the statement goes on to indi-

[1] Dhorme, *Les Religions de Babylonie et d'Assyrie*, 285.
[2] Meissner, *op. cit.*, II, 248.

cate misfortune for Gutium and Akkad respectively when the same phenomenon occurred on the twenty-ninth or the thirtieth day of the month. Another celestial event to be watched with care was the appearance of the sun and moon together in the sky. This might happen on any day between the twelfth and the twentieth of the month, and the omen differed according to the day on which it occurred. The following are some of the omens drawn from this event:

"If the sun and moon are seen together on the twelfth day, it betokens the end of the dynasty, destruction for men, the robber will cut off the head; if the moon and sun are seen together on the thirteenth day, it betokens unrest, trade and commerce in the land will not prosper, the foot of the enemy will be in the land, the enemy will take everything away from the land; if the moon and sun are seen together on the fourteenth day, it betokens prosperity, the heart of the land will be of good cheer, the gods will think of Akkad with favor, men will rejoice, the cattle of Akkad will lie down in the fields in peace."[3] The list continues to enumerate the omens for the remaining days up to the twentieth.

An event of particularly ill omen was the eclipse of the moon, in explanation of which a special myth had arisen. This is Mr. Gadd's account of it: "Enlil had appointed Sin, Shamash, and Ishtar to guide the heavens aright, but the Seven (Devils) set upon the Moon-god and surrounded him. Thus an eclipse was brought about amid the consternation of the gods. Enlil saw the distress of Sin and sent his messenger Nusku to bring the alarming news to Ea, whom we already know as the master of incantation. When Ea heard this in the Ocean his mouth was filled with lamentation and he bit his lip. Then follows the conventional scene which is reproduced in so many incantations—Ea sends his son Marduk to see the evil that has been wrought, or the ill from which a sick man is suffering; Marduk returns with a report and asks the advice of his father, who after repeat-

[3] Meissner, *op. cit.*, II, 248–49.

ing a polite formula signifying that Marduk already possesses all knowledge, details the magical means that are to be used for the remedy of the ill disposition. A regular ingredient in the incantations is the identifying of the priest with Ea, so that his words and actions become symbolically those of the god himself."[4] The myth, it is clear, is part of the incantation and its accompanying ritual by the power of which the imprisoned Moon-god was released and the eclipse brought to an end. Naturally, an eclipse of the moon, besides being of great importance as a source of omens, was also an occasion of special rituals intended to avert from the city or the state any evils which the eclipse might threaten. Here are some extracts from a ritual tablet relating to an eclipse of the moon: "On the day of the eclipse of the moon, the priests of the houses of the gods of Tiranna shall place a *garakku* (altar) in the gate of the house of their gods. When the light fails they should cry aloud that catastrophe, murder, rebellion and eclipse come not near to Erech, the palace, the shrine of Eanna, and the houses of the gods of Tiranna. For a lamentation they should raise their cry. Until the eclipse is clear they should cry aloud."[5] One element of the eclipse ritual was the bringing of sacred musical instruments out of the temples: "On the day of the eclipse of the moon, they should bring out of the house the copper *halhallatu* (some kind of flute or trumpet), the copper *ershemma* (possibly the sacred harp), and the copper *lilissu* (the sacred drum)."[6] The last of these was peculiarly sacred, indeed treated as a god, and was evidently brought out to reassure the public at times of eclipse or abnormal darkness.

Returning to the ominous character of the eclipse of the moon, we find that omens varied according to the month and the time of night when the eclipse took place. Thus: "If an eclipse takes place in Nisan, in the first watch, there will be destruction,

[4] Hooke, *Myth and Ritual*, 65.
[5] *Ritual for the Observance of Eclipses*, B.R., 4, No. 6.
[6] *Id.*

and brother will slay brother. If it happens in Iyyar, the king will die, and the king's son will not succeed to his father's throne. If it happens in Tammuz, agriculture will prosper and prices will rise. If it happens in Ab, Adad will send a flood upon the land,"[7] and so forth. Many letters in the correspondence of the Assyrian kings are concerned with the reports from the royal astrologers concerning eclipses and other aspects of the moon's appearance, and the omens arising therefrom.

But the moon was not the only source of omens; although the sun was not so important in this respect as the moon, nevertheless it was carefully watched; its eclipses and its color at the time of rising or setting, were the occasion of omens. Solar eclipses were almost uniformly of evil omen. Other planets were also important for divination, especially Venus whose Babylonian name was Dilbat. The heliacal rising and setting of this planet were carefully watched and yielded many omens. Thus: "When Venus disappears on the twelfth of Kislev at sunrise and remains hidden for two months and four days, and then reappears on the sixteenth of Shebat at sunrise, this signifies that agriculture will be prosperous."[8] Jupiter, or *Nebiru*, Marduk's planet, was mainly a source of favorable omens, as also was Saturn. The fixed stars, comets, and meteors, were also the source of omens. We have a late Babylonian text in which the influence of specified stars upon every possible situation in daily life is recorded. Hence arose the firm belief of the general public in the influence of the stars and celestial bodies upon birth and the future of the individual, and the practice of resorting to diviners for the preparation of horoscopes, a practice which spread all over the west and has persisted till the present day.

Lastly, we come to the weather omens which in general were believed to be under the control of Adad. The significance of thunder depended upon the month in which it was heard and the timbre of its sound; "When Adad causes his voice to be

---

[7] Meissner, *op. cit.*, II, 249.
[8] Meissner, *op. cit.*, II, 254.

heard in Nisan, the rule of the enemy will cease; when it happens in Tammuz, agriculture will prosper; when it happens in Adar, the land will revolt from the king; when it thunders like a great dog, the *ummanmanda* (i.e., the Scythians) will arise who have no rival; when it thunders like a lion, a king will fall,"[9] and so on. The significance of lightning lay in the quarter of the heavens in which it was seen: "When there is lightning by night in the South, Adad will cause floods; when there is lightning by night in the North, Adad will flood the land of Gutium,"[10] and so on for each quarter of the compass. Rain also had significance according to the day of the month on which it fell, while earthquakes were always of disastrous import. A rainbow over the city was of good omen for the city, the king, and the nobles.

[9] *Id., op. cit.*, II, 258.
[10] *Id., op. cit.*, II, 258.

CHAPTER X

THE GODS AND THE MORAL
GOVERNMENT OF THE WORLD

MUCH of what we have gathered so far concerning the religion of the Babylonians and the Assyrians would seem to suggest that it consisted mainly in the mechanical performance of an elaborate system of ritual which shaped and directed the life of the individual from the cradle to the grave. In the ancient myths the gods behave like men; they eat and drink, quarrel and deceive, are jealous of one another, and cannot be said to possess any moral standards. Yet this judgment requires some qualification. In the proemium to the Code of Hammurabi the great king is represented as saying: "At that time, Anu and Bel called me, Hammurabi, the exalted prince, who fears the gods, to make righteousness prevail in the land, to destroy the wicked and the evil, to prevent the strong from oppressing the weak." Here we have, about the middle of the eighteenth millennium B.C., a clear statement that the high gods are animated by a moral purpose, and that the moral standards set forth in the Code represent the will of the gods. Still earlier traces of a moral conception of the duties of kingship are to be found in the inscriptions of the reforming king of Lagash, Urukagina, about 2000 B.C. This king represents himself as deputed by his god Ningirsu to put an end to the rapacity of priests and officials which had become rampant during the reigns of his predecessors; how far such an attitude was general during the Sumerian period there is not evidence to show. It may be possible, as von Soden suggests,[1] to see a religious motive behind the determination of the Assyrian kings to bring the whole known world into subjection to their god Ashur.

After the fall of the old Babylonian kingdom there seems to be evidence of a change of attitude in the minds of the priests

[1] Z.D.M.G. N.F., Bd. 14, 11 ft. 2, p. 152.

towards the non-moral conception of the gods found in the old Sumerian myths. It is possible that something like the prophetic editing of the early history of Israel may be found in the re-editing of the Epic of Creation, and the suppression of many of the more unedifying Sumerian myths about the gods. The experience of a prolonged foreign domination seems to have raised in the minds of thoughtful Babylonians the question why their gods had allowed this to happen to them; just as the Assyrian domination of Israel raised the same question in the minds of the Hebrew prophets. To both questions the same answer was given or arrived at: that such disasters were a punishment for sin.

Here we must pause for a moment to inquire into the Babylonian conception of sin. In such collections of incantations as *maqlu* and *shurpu*, of which mention has already been made (see p. 74), frequent confessions of sin are to be found, and while it is clear that in general, for the ordinary Babylonian, sin meant some failure in cult observance, some breach of a taboo, by which the sufferer had unwittingly brought upon himself the anger of the gods or put himself into the power of malignant demons, it also appears from the same texts that the supplicant is conscious of having committed moral offenses, especially those against family ties and duties; also untruthfulness and lack of clemency are mentioned. Further, passages in prayers and hymns to various gods occur in which there is expressed a strong sense that sin has caused a breach between the supplicant and his god. For example, in a prayer to Ishtar, we find the following: "To thee have I prayed; forgive my debt. Forgive my sin, my iniquity, my shameful deeds, and my offense. Overlook my shameful deeds; accept my prayer; loosen my fetters; secure my deliverance."[2] Again, in a remarkable prayer addressed to all the gods, known or unknown, belonging probably to the time of Ashurbanipal, we find the expression of the sense that man cannot know the will of the gods and cannot therefore know whether he is committing sin; this is made the ground for

[2] Pritchard, *op. cit.*, 385.

a plea for mercy. Here is an excerpt from it: "Man is dumb; he knows nothing; Mankind, everyone that exists, what does he know? Whether he is committing sin or doing good, he does not even know. O my lord, do not cast thy servant down; he is plunged into the waters of a swamp; take him by the hand. The sin which I have done, turn into goodness; the transgression which I have committed, let the wind carry away; my many misdeeds strip off like a garment. . . . Remove my transgressions and I will sing thy praise. May thy heart, like the heart of a real mother, be quieted toward me; like a real mother and a real father may it be quieted toward me."[3] Nevertheless, it must also be pointed out that in the same prayer the supplicant tells the god that he has eaten forbidden food without knowing it, and has trodden upon forbidden ground unwittingly. Hence it would seem that no sharp distinction existed in the mind of the Babylonian of the eighth century B.C. between the two kinds of sin, and that both kinds might be felt to be the cause, not merely of sickness and disaster, but also of a breach between a man and his god.

It is also necessary to point out here that the Babylonian conception of divine retribution for sin and reward for righteousness was entirely confined to this life, just as we find it in the earlier Hebrew conceptions of reward and punishment. The Egyptian conception of the afterlife included the belief in a judgment after death, and a blessed immortality in the realm of Osiris for those who came through the ordeal successfully. Later Jewish thought developed a similar outlook, although of a more spiritual character; but, so far as the available evidence shows, the Babylonian conception of the afterlife remained to the end a gloomy and forbidding one. The description given to Gilgamesh by his friend Enkidu when he was allowed to return to the upper world, of the state of the dead in the underworld, seems to have continued unchanged, and may have been the source of the early Hebrew and Greek ideas of the afterlife.

[3] Pritchard, *op. cit.*, 392.

Enkidu tells Gilgamesh that the body he had known and loved is devoured by vermin and filled with dust. Also, earlier in the Epic, Enkidu sees in a dream the state of the dead, and tells his dream to Gilgamesh: "He (i.e., the god of the underworld) transformed me, so that my arms were like those of a bird. Looking at me, he leads me to the House of Darkness, the abode of Irkalla, to the house which none leave who have entered it, on the road from which there is no way back, to the house wherein the dwellers are bereft of light, where dust is their fare and clay their food. They are clothed like birds, with wings for garments, and see no light, residing in darkness."[4]

The early myths show how much the Sumerians and Babylonians were preoccupied with the problem of why the gods had allowed death and disease to enter the world, and the conventional answer seems to have been that the gods were jealous of man, and had kept immortality for themselves, leaving death to be the lot of man.

After the conception of the gods had become moralized, the common view of the gods' government of the world was that they were supposed to reward virtue and punish sin with the material rewards and penalties of prosperity and long life or disaster and death. This, as we know, was also the conventional view among the Hebrews, as exemplified in the discourses of Job's friends. But doubts about the validity of this assumption seem to have arisen among the Babylonians much earlier than they did among the Hebrews. As early as the end of the second millennium B.C. someone wrote a hymn to Marduk, known by its opening words, *ludlul bel nimeqi*, "I will praise the lord of wisdom." In this remarkable piece of Babylonian literature, sometimes called "The Babylonian Job," the problem of the moral government of the world is raised. The author, who represents himself as being an official of high rank, describes how, in spite of all his piety and scrupulous observance of his religious duties, he was pursued by misfortune and afflicted by disease.

[4] Pritchard, *op. cit.*, 87, 99.

As he contemplates his sad state, he is compelled to cry out, "What is good in one's sight is evil for a god; what is bad in one's own mind is good for his god. Who can understand the counsel of the gods in the midst of heaven? The plan of a god is deep waters, who can comprehend it?"[5] His condition grows worse; no diviner or exorcist can help him; no god comes to his aid, no goddess takes his hand in mercy; he has come to the river of the underworld, when suddenly Marduk intervenes, draws him out of Hubur, the underworld river, and restores him to health and prosperity, so that all who see it wonder and praise Marduk.

As in the Hebrew Job so here there is a double answer. The Hebrew poet at the end of the poetic part of his work, leaves Job with the crushing sense of his own insignificance and inability to understand the smallest part of the ways of Yahweh. He ends with a confession of his own moral unworthiness, but with his intellectual problem unsolved. But, if the closing chapter is accepted as part of the original intention of the poet, he gives his readers the conventional happy ending. Job is healed and his prosperity restored twofold, and he is seen offering sacrifices to Yahweh. Similarly, the Babylonian poet represents the sufferer as coming to the conclusion that the ways of the gods are unsearchable, but nevertheless shows Marduk as finally coming to his help and restoring him to health and prosperity, although no explanation of why he had been allowed to suffer is provided.

A second, somewhat later text, in the form of a dialogue between a master and his slave, goes much further in its devastating skepticism and denial of all moral values. It offers many remarkable parallels to the book of Ecclesiastes. The end of the text is missing, so we cannot know whether it would have ended on the same note of unrelieved pessimism.

This skeptical strand in Hebrew religious thought could not stifle the deeper current of spiritual experience fed by the prophets which found expression in such conceptions as that of the Suffering Servant in Deutero-Isaiah, and flowed on to its

[5] *Id., op. cit.*, 435.

consummation in Christianity. But there is no parallel to this in the development of Babylonian religion. The inherent contradiction between the conception of gods possessing a moral will, and the elaborate system of ritual observances intended to induce the gods to do their moral duty, so to speak, was never resolved, and Babylonian religion was finally overwhelmed under the weight of a crushing mass of unintelligible tradition.

APPENDIX

AN appendix is here added containing a selection of ritual
and other religious texts from various sources illustrating the
account of Babylonian and Assyrian religion given in the previous pages:

(1) *Ritual Texts:*
Ritual of the Babylonian New Year Festival.

"In the month Nisan, on the second day, two hours before
the end of the night, the *urigallu* (see p. 45) shall rise and wash
himself with water from the river; he shall go in before Bel,
then he shall put on a linen garment; he shall say this prayer
before Bel:

> Bel, without equal in his anger;
> Bel, merciful king, lord of the lands,
> Causing the great gods to be favorably disposed;
> Bel, whose glance overthrows the mighty;
> Lord of kings, light of mankind, fixer of destinies.
> Bel, Babel is thy seat, Borsippa is thy crown.
> The wide heavens compose thy liver;
> Bel, with thine eyes thou dost behold the universe;
> With thine oracles thou dost control the oracles;
> With thy glance thou dost give the law;
> With thine arms thou dost crush the mighty;
> Thy . . . thou dost grasp with thine hand;
> When thou dost see them thou dost take pity on them;
> Thou causest them to see the light; they declare thy might.
> Lord of the lands, light of the Igigi, who dost bestow blessing;
> Who will not speak of thee? Who will not declare thy
> might?

Who will not tell of thy glory? Who will not praise thy
    kingdom?
Lord of the lands, whose dwelling is in E-ud-ul; who dost
    take the hand of him (who has fallen);
Have mercy on thy city, Babel!
Turn thy face toward thy temple, Esagila!
Establish the liberty of the children of Babel, objects of
    (thy) protection!

"The number of the lines (i.e., of the above prayer) is 21.
It is the secret of Esagila. No one save the *urigallu* of E-kua
shall see it.

"After he has said this prayer he shall open the door: the
priests shall rise: they shall carry out their customary rituals
before Bel and Beltia (i.e., Marduk and his consort, Zarpanit)."

Then follows a lacuna and a passage which is too broken to
allow of connected translation, but it indicates that, still on the
second day, the *urigallu* did something with the crown of Anu,
and recited a prayer three times. The text resumes with the
ritual for the third day.

"In the month Nisan, on the third day, . . . (the *urigallu*)
shall rise; he shall wash himself . . . he shall say this prayer to
Bel; (only fragments of the prayer remain). He shall open the
doors. (All the priests) shall enter; they shall carry out (their
customary rituals). The *kalû*-priests (see p. 45) and the singers
likewise . . . (*lacuna of three lines*). When it is three hours after
sunrise he shall summon a craftsman; then he shall give him
precious stones and gold from the treasury of Marduk for the
making of two images for the sixth day. He shall summon a
carpenter, and shall give him cedarwood and tamarisk wood.
He shall summon a jeweler, and shall give him gold. During the
third to the sixth day from the offerings placed before Bel—for
the craftsman of the shoulder (?) (of the victim), for the jeweler
the breast, for the carpenter the thigh, for the weaver the ribs—

this is what they shall bring for the workmen to the *urigallu* of E-kua from the offerings placed before Bel.

"As for these images, they are seven fingers high. One is made of cedarwood, the other of tamarisk wood. They are overlaid with a shekel's weight of gold. They are adorned with precious stones. The one holds in his left hand a serpent made of cedarwood, and raises his right hand to Nebo; the other holds in his left hand a scorpion, and raises his right hand to Nebo. They are clothed with red garments, and their loins are girded with a palm branch. Until the sixth day they shall be placed in the temple of the god Daian (i.e., the Judge). Loaves from the table of the god Daian shall be offered to them. On the sixth day, when Nebo arrives at Ehursagtila, the executioner shall cut off their heads; then a fire shall be kindled before Nebo, and they shall be thrown into the fire.

"In the month Nisan, on the fourth day, three and a third hours before the end of the night, the *urigallu* shall rise, and wash himself with water from the river; he shall put on a linen garment; before Bel and Beltia . . . he shall address this incantation to Bel; he shall utter this prayer to Bel:

Most mighty lord of the Igigi, most exalted of the great gods,
Lord of the regions, king of the gods, Marduk, who dost fix
 the destinies,
Glorious, exalted, most high prince;
Who holdest the kingship, possessest the lordship;
Gleaming light, Marduk dwelling in E-ud-ul;
Who dost overwhelm with a flood the land of the enemies.
(*Lacuna of four lines*)
Who dost pass through the heavens, dost heap up the earth;
Who dost measure the waters of the sea, who dost cause (the
 fields) to be tilled;
Dwelling in E-ud-ul, Marduk the exalted;
Fixing the destinies of all the gods;

Who givest the holy scepter to the king who fears thee.
I am the *urigallu* of E-kua who blesses thee;
Be gracious to thy city, Babel;
Have mercy on thy temple, Esagila!
At thy exalted word, lord of the great gods,
May the light shine upon the children of Babel!

He shall go out from before Bel, then he shall recite this prayer to Beltia:

She is mighty, she is divine, she is exalted among the god-
desses;
Zarpanit, the brightest of the stars, dwelling in E-ud-ul;
The . . . of the goddesses, clothed with light;
Who dost pass through the heavens, dost heap up the earth;
Zarpanit whose dwelling is exalted;
Shining Beltia, exalted and most high;
Among the goddesses there is none like her;
She accuses and intercedes.
She abases the rich and vindicates the cause of the lowly;
She overthrows the enemy, he who does not revere her god-
head;
She delivers the captive, and takes the hand of the fallen;
Bless the servant who honors thy name;
Fix the destiny of the king who fears thee;
Give life to the children of Babel, thy dependents;
Plead for them before Marduk, the king of the gods;
Let them tell of thy glory, let them exalt thy kingdom;
Let them speak of thy prowess, let them glorify thy name;
Have mercy on thy servant who blesses thee;
Take his hand in need and suffering;
In disease and distress give him life;
May he go ever in joy and delight;
May he tell thy prowess to the peoples of the whole world.

He shall go out into the great court, and shall take up his stand facing the north; he shall bless Esagila three times with these words:

Star Iku, Esagila, image of heaven and earth!
He shall open the doors; all the priests shall enter; they shall
carry out their customary rituals; likewise the *kalû*-priests and
the singers. When he has done that, after the little meal at the
end of the day, the *urigallu* of E-kua shall recite to Bel *Enuma
Elish* (i.e., the Creation Epic) from beginning to end. While he
is reciting *Enuma Elish* to Bel, the crown of Anu and the throne
of Enlil shall remain covered.

"In the month Nisan, on the fifth day, four hours before the
end of the night, the *urigallu* shall rise, and shall wash himself
with water from the river, with water from the Tigris and the
Euphrates; he shall go in before Bel, and shall clothe himself
with a linen garment; he shall recite this prayer before Bel and
Beltia:

(*The first twelve lines are imperfectly preserved*)

My lord is Dimmer-an-ki-a (the name borne by Marduk in
    the chamber of destinies); my lord be appeased!
My lord is the star Mu-sir-kesh-da (the Dragon), who holds
    the scepter and the ring; my lord, be appeased!
My lord is the star of Eridu (the Ship), who possesses wis-
    dom; my lord, be appeased!
(The following twenty-five lines invoke Bel and Beltia (i.e.,
    Marduk and Zarpanit) by the names of stars.)

After he has said this prayer he shall open the doors; all the
priests shall enter, and shall carry out their customary rituals;
likewise the *kalû*-priests and the singers. Two hours after sunrise, when the table of Bel and Beltia has been set in order, the
urigallu shall summon a *mashmashu* (an exorcist) who shall
purify the temple. Then he shall sprinkle the temple with water
from the reservoir of the Tigris and from that of the Euphrates.
He shall sound the bronze *lilissu* (the sacred drum) in the midst
of the temple. He shall bring the censer and the torch into the
midst of the temple. The exorcist shall remain in the midst of
the court. He shall not enter into the chapel of Bel and Beltia.

When the purification of the temple (of Bel) is completed, he shall enter into Ezida, the chapel of Nebo; then with the censer, the torch, and the water pot, he shall purify the temple and chapel of Nebo, and shall sprinkle them with water from the reservoir of the Tigris and the Euphrates. He shall touch all the doors of the chapel with cedar oil. In the midst of the court of the chapel he shall place a silver censer upon which he shall mingle incense and cypress. He shall summon an executioner who shall cut off the head of a sheep; then with the carcass of the sheep the exorcist shall wipe the temple; he shall recite spells to exorcise the temple. He shall purify the chapel throughout its entire extent; then he shall remove the censer. The exorcist shall remove the carcass of that sheep; he shall go to the river, and standing with his face to the west he shall cast the carcass of the sheep into the river. He shall go out into the country. The executioner shall do the same with the head of the sheep. The executioner and the exorcist shall go out into the country. So long as Nebo is in Babel they shall not come into Babel; from the fifth to the twelfth day they shall stay in the country. The *urigallu* of E-kua shall not see the purifying of the temple. If he sees it, he is not clean. After the purification of the temple, when it is three and a third hours after sunrise, the *urigallu* of E-kua shall go out of the chapel, and shall summon all the craftsmen. They shall take out the golden heaven (see p. 43) from the treasury of Marduk; then they shall cover Ezida, the chapel of Nebo, from the roof (?) to the foundations. The *urigallu* of E-kua and the craftsmen shall recite this invocation:

> They shall purify the temple.
> Marduk, child of Eridu, dwelling in E-ud-ul,
> Azag-sug, god who dost sprinkle with pure water;
> Nin-a-ha-du, who hearest prayers;
> Marduk will purify the temple;
> Azag-sug, will draw the design:
> Nin-a-ha-du will set in motion the spell.

Begone, all evil that is within the temple!
May Bel destroy thee, great demon!
Be cut off from the place where thou art!

All the craftsmen shall go out of the gate. At . . . of the day, the *urigallu* shall go in before Bel; he shall set in order before Bel a golden table of offerings; he shall place roast meats thereon; he shall place twelve (loaves) of the regular offering thereon; he shall fill a golden . . . with salt, and shall place it on the table; then he shall fill a golden (pot) with honey, and shall place it on the table; he shall place four golden jars on the table; he shall place a golden censer before the table; (he shall place) incense and cypress upon it; he shall pour out wine; he shall recite this prayer:

Marduk, lord, exalted among the gods,
Dwelling in Esagila, creator of the laws,
Who . . . to the great gods;
. . . I praise thy might.
May thy heart turn towards him who takes thy hand!
In Ezur, the house of prayer,
In the . . . your place, may he lift up his head!

When he has said this, he shall take away the table; he shall summon the craftsmen together; he shall deliver the table with all that is on it to the craftsmen, and shall cause them to carry it to Nebo; the craftsmen shall take it; they shall go in the . . . to the bank of the canal; when Nebo arrives at . . . they shall set it up for Nebo; when they have placed the table before Nebo, while Nebo is getting out of the ship Id-da-he-du, they shall offer the loaves of the table; then they shall place on the table water to wash the hands of the king. Then they shall conduct the king into Esagila; the craftsmen shall go out of the gate. When the king has come in before Bel, the *urigallu* shall come out of the chapel; then he shall receive from the hands of the king the scepter, the ring, and the *harpé* (ceremonial weapon); he shall take his royal crown; he shall bring these things in before Bel, and shall place them on a seat before Bel. He shall come out of the chapel; he shall strike the king's cheek; he shall place . . . behind him; he shall bring him before Bel; he shall pull his ears; he shall make him kneel on the ground; the king shall repeat the following (words) once:

> I have not sinned, lord of the countries; I have not despised thy divinity;
> I have not destroyed Babel; I have not caused it to be scattered;
> I have not shaken Esagila; I have not forgotten its rituals;
> I have not smitten suppliants on the cheek;
> I have not humiliated them;
> I care for Babel; I have not broken down its walls.

(There follows a lacuna of five lines containing the end of the king's confession and the beginning of the *urigallu's* address to the king which continues somewhat broken):

> Fear not . . .
> Bel has said . . .
> Bel will hear thy prayer . . .
> He will exalt thy kingship . . .
> He will magnify thy rule . . .
> On the day of the feast of the new moon thou shalt . . .
> On the feast of the opening of the gate purify thy hands;
> Night and day . . .
> Thou who . . . Babel, his city;
> Who . . . Esagila, his temple;
> Who . . . the children of Babel, the suppliants;
> Bel shall bless thee for ever;
> He will destroy thy enemies, he will beat down thine adversaries.

When the *urigallu* has spoken thus, the king shall resume the usual glory of his appearance. The *urigallu* shall bring out of the chapel the scepter, the ring, the *harpé*, and the crown, and shall restore them to the king; he shall strike the king on the cheek; when he has smitten his cheek and tears come, Bel is favorable; if his tears do not come, Bel is angry; the enemy will arise and bring about his downfall.

"When he has done this, forty minutes after sunset, the *urigallu* shall bind together forty reeds, of three ells each in length, neither split nor broken, but straight, bound together with a palm branch. They shall dig a trench in the great court; then he shall place the reeds in that trench; he shall place in it honey, cream, and oil of the best quality; he shall place a white bull before the trench. The king with a reed shall kindle a flame in the midst of the trench; the king and the *urigallu* shall recite this prayer:

> O divine Bull, shining light who dost illumine the darkness,
> Burning Bull of Anu . . .
> O Gibil (the fire-god) . . ."

Here unfortunately our text breaks off. From scattered allusions in other texts it is possible to infer that the ritual last described was preparatory to the king's "taking the hand" of Marduk, to lead him to the *akitu*, a temple situated outside Babylon, to the north of the city, where certain very important parts of the New Year ritual were carried out. The journey to the *akitu* proceeded partly by the *Aibur-shabu*, or sacred way, leaving Babylon by the great Ishtar gate, and partly in the sacred ship along the Arakhtu canal, a branch of the Euphrates. The ceremony known as "the fixing of destinies" took place in a *parakku*, or chapel, apparently situated in Ezida, the shrine of Nebo, in Marduk's temple Esagila. Nebo had his own temple Ezida in Borsippa, not to be confused with the place where the ceremony was performed. The precise form in which the ritual of the fixing of destinies was carried out is not known to us. From other sources we learn that Marduk was in the *parakku* of destinies on the eighth day of the festival, and it is probable that the ceremony took place on that day.

(2) *Ritual Commentary*

This text, badly preserved, belongs to the class of texts known as ritual commentaries, of which we have only a few examples. It is intended for the use of priests officiating at the New Year Festival at Babylon, and explains each detail of the ritual by a reference to some element in the mythology. It gives some information about the proceedings which took place on the remaining six days of the festival which are wanting in the text given above.

". . . that is Bel who is shut up in the mountain (probably Etemenanki, the ziqqurat of Babylon) . . . he brings him forth. A messenger runs from his lord (saying) 'Who will bring him forth?' He . . . who goes and brings him forth. He . . . who rides; that is he who goes to the mountain. To which . . . he goes; that is the house on the edge (lit. 'lip') of the mountain in which they question him. Nebo who comes from Borsippa, that is he who comes for the safety of his father (Marduk) who is held captive. The . . . who run through the streets; they seek for Bel, (saying) 'Where is he held captive?' The (goddess, probably Zarpanit, Marduk's consort) who stretches out her hands; she prays to Sin and Shamash, 'Cause Bel to live.' The gate to which she comes (is) the gate of the grave, she enters and seeks him . . . the two who stand at the door of Esagila (are) his guards, they are placed over him to guard him . . . are made, after the gods had shut him up; he has disappeared from life, to the house of bondage from sun and light they have brought him down . . . which come near unto him, which clothe him, (are) wounds with which he was wounded in his blood; the goddess who remains with him, for his safety has come; the son of Ashur who goes not with him says, 'I am not a transgressor, I shall not be slain', . . . Ashur, my judgment is open before him, he will judge my cause . . . who goes not with him, that son of Ashur, he is the watcher appointed over him, he watches before the fortress; that which is bound on the canopy of the Lady of Babylon (is) the head of the transgressor who (went down) with him; they slew him, his head is bound on the (canopy) of the Lady of Babylon . . . who went and returned to Borsippa, the canopy in which he is . . . (after) Bel has come into the mountain the city is in confusion on account of him; battle has taken place within it; the pig (sty) in the way of Nebo when he comes from Borsippa to do homage, Nebo when he comes, stands before it, looks upon it; the transgressor who was with Bel is that, when he looks upon him who was with Bel. The exorcists who go before him should repeat the incantation, they are his people who mourn for him. The *mahhu*-priest who goes before the Lady of Babylon, he is the messenger who weeps before her (saying), 'They have brought him into the mountain.' She cries out thus, 'My brother, my brother!' His garments which they bring to the Lady of Erech, his adornments (?) which they bring, either silver, or gold, or precious stones, which they bring from Esagila to the temples, that is his house. The . . . with which he is clothed in . . . the milk which they . . . before Ishtar of Nineveh, because she nourished him, they show favor to her. *Enuma Elish* (the Creation Epic) which they recite before Bel in Nisan, they sing it because he is imprisoned. They pray their prayers, they make their entreaties . . . it is; he says thus, 'The good deeds of Ashur, these have I done,' and, 'What is my sin?' He (who looks to heaven, to Sin and) Shamash he prays, 'Let me live'; he who looks to the earth . . . that he may come out of the mountain. (He who is with) Bel does not go forth to the *akitu*-temple . . . of a prisoner he bears; he sits with him. The Lady of Babylon who (carries) black wool behind her and spotted wool in front of her . . . with her hands, blood from the heart which has been shed. Who on the eighth of Nisan before they slaughter the pig, that mistress of the house asks 'Who is the transgressor?' . . . they bring, the transgressor they slay . . . in the month of Nisan they make much meal because he is a prisoner. The hand water which they offer, (of which they say) it removes the plague; the *sheritu*-garment which is upon him, (of which) they say, 'That water, it is sickness.' That one, within, recites *Enuma Elish*; when heaven and earth were not created, then Anshar came into being, when he made city and temple, then water came into being, which is over against Anshar . . . He whose transgression is within . . . the water . . . The footrace which took place in the month of Nisan before Bel and the cities . . . when Ashur sent out Ninurta for the conquest of Zu (see p. 70). He says before Ashur, 'Zu is defeated.' Ashur says to . . . go, tell it to all the gods. He told them and they rejoiced at it."

The above translation is based on Zimmern's reconstruction and translation of the ritual commentary in tablet VAT 9555. It will be seen that, in spite of much obscurity, due to the imperfect preservation of the text, a number of interesting details are added to our knowledge of what took place during the eleven days of the festival.

(3) *Ritual Commentary*

"Bel is shut up in the mountain . . . brings him forth; a messenger runs from his lord saying, 'Who will bring him forth?' . . . will go and bring him forth . . . who rides, to that mountain he comes.

"Bel . . . who goes to the well, stands at the well, performs worship at the well . . . (who) for Bel threw it (or him) into the abyss, gave it (or him) up to the Anunnaki. The fire which is kindled, that is Marduk, when he in his childhood . . . who throw high the burning arrows, those are the gods, his father and his brothers when they heard . . . brings up, and (whom) the gods kiss, that is Marduk, when Belit in his childhood brought him up and they kissed him. The fire that burns before Belit, the sheep which they place on the brazier, that is Kingu, when they burnt him with fire. The burning arrows which they kindle at the brazier (these are) the unescapable (implacable) arrows from the quiver of Bel which in their throwing are full of terror, in their throwing slay the mighty, are stained with blood and dirt; they sprinkle the mountain; the gods come hither, his father, his brothers; the hostile gods, Zu, Ashakku, are overthrown by them; the king, who holds a *dumaki* (weapon?) over himself and burns a kid, that is Marduk who held his weapon over himself and burnt the children of Bel and Ea in the fire. The king who breaks a vessel with a hammer (?), that is Marduk when he. . . . The king who causes the baked bread of the priest to leap with him, that is Marduk and Nebo who . . . Anu prevailed against him and destroyed him. The king who stands by the doorpost (?) . . . is laid in the king's hand while a singing-priest chants, 'Namurritu,' that is Marduk who . . . his feet lay within Ea's while Dilbat (Venus) passed before him . . . which he causes to leap, that is the inside of Ea's temple when he overcame with his hands . . . the warrior who holds a sweet fig in his hand; the . . . who take his hand, brings him in before the god, so that he shows the sweet fig to the god and the king, that is . . . whom they send to Bel, who . . . him, and takes Nergal by the hand, who entered Esagila, showed the weapons of his hands to Marduk the king of the gods, and Zarpanit, which they then kiss and bless. The *kurgaru*-priests who sport in the field, make merry, throw burning arrows, (kindle) firebrands, who lift one another, use violence, that is the . . . who raise a cry before Bel and Ea, cast looks of fear towards them, their . . . cut off, (throw) into the abyss." (Remainder unintelligible.)

The above translation is based on Zimmern's reconstruction and translation of the ritual commentary contained in K. 3476, probably referring to the New Year Festival. The following fragmentary text, also from Zimmern, refers to Marduk in the *parakku* of destiny:

(4) *Ritual Chant*

"This is that which the *asinnu*-priests should recite:

'(Bel and Belit) of the lands, in E-esh-mah, I have looked
    towards you;

With torches I have lighted your way.'

"As soon as Bel is seated in the *parakku* of destiny this should
be said:

'Set forth, Bel, the king awaits thee;

Set forth, our lady, the king awaits thee;

The lord sets forth from Babylon, the lands bow before him;

Zarpanit sets forth. . . .' "

(5) *Exorcism-text*

Extract from Tablet IV of the *maqlu*-series (ed. G. Meier,
1937).

"Incantation, Boil, boil, burn, burn!

Evil and wicked, come not near, begone!

Who art thou, whose son? Who art thou, whose daughter?

Who sit and your witchcraft and your spells

Against me weave?

May Ea, the magician, free me,

May he bring to nought your sorceries.

Ashariludu (Marduk), the magician of the gods, the son of
    Ea, the wise one.

I fetter you, I bind you, I deliver you

To Gira, who scorches, burns, fetters,

Seizes the sorceresses.

May Gira, the burning one, strengthen my arms!

Witchcraft, rebellion, the evil word, love, hate,

Perversion of justice, murder, paralysis of the mouth,

Tearing of the bowels, burning of the face, and madness,

(With these) have you bewitched me, caused me to be be-
    witched:

May Gira free me!

You have chosen me for a corpse,

You have handed me over to a skull,
You have delivered me into the power of a family ghost,
You have delivered me into the power of a strange ghost,
To a wandering ghost that has no guardian,
To a ghost inhabiting fallen ruins,
Have you handed me over;
To the desert, to the uninhabited land, to the waste land,
  have you handed me over;
To the walls and fortifications have you handed me over;
To the goddess of the desert and the high places you have
  handed me over;
To the oven, the hearth, the furnace, and the bellows, you
  have handed me over;
You have handed over my image into the power of a corpse."
The tablet continues in this strain for many lines, describing
what the sorceress has done with the image of the suppliant who
is supposed to be using this form of exorcism to obtain deliverance from the spells of the witch. This section of the incantation
closes with an invocation:

"I have bound you, I have fettered you, I have handed you
  over
To Gira, who scorches, burns, binds, seizes the witches.
May the burning Gira undo your knots (i.e. spells),
Annul your incantations, (untie) your cord,
By the command of Marduk, the son of Ea, the wise one,
And of Gira, the burning one, the son of Anu, the mighty
  one."

The continuation shows that the sufferer from the machinations
of the witch adopted the sorcerer's technique and made an
image, or images, of the witch, or witches, by whose spells he
had been afflicted. These images were devoted to Gira and Gibil,
the fire-gods, by being thrown into an oven or furnace. Also
magic knots, representing the witch's spells, were untied in order
to free the sufferer from the effects of the spells.

(6) *Ritual of the Washing of the Mouth*

This is a ritual used for the consecration and installation of a new or restored statue of a god. It is of particular interest because of its resemblance to a similar ritual performed in Egypt for the purpose of giving life to a portrait statue. The translation here given is that published by Professor Sidney Smith in the *Journal of the Royal Asiatic Society*, January 1925:

"When you have to 'wash the mouth' of a god, on a favorable day you should set two pots of holy water in the workshop. (Place) a red cloth in front of the god and a white cloth beside the god. Prepare offerings for Ea and Marduk. Perform the washing of the mouth of that god and then prepare the offering for that god. Raise your hand and repeat three times the incantation: 'Thou who art born in heaven from its wind.' Repeat three times the incantation: 'From this time forth thou shalt go before thy father Ea' before that god, and then take the hand of the god and cause him to (lead) a ram. Repeat the incantation: 'In thy going forth, in thy going forth, coming from the grove,' (as you proceed) from the house of the craftsmen, with torches, before that god, to the river bank, and then seat him on a reed mat, and then turn his face to the east. Set a canopy. Prepare offerings for Ea, Marduk, and that god. Pour out a libation of the best beer, with meal. (Flay) the skin of the ram. Place a bronze axe, a bronze pick, a bronze *takkame*, a *balgu-fish*, and a tortoise of silver and gold therein. Wrap up and then throw into the river. Say 'O King, Lord of the Deep' three times before Ea, and then raise your hand and repeat three times the incantation 'Ea, King of the Abyss,' and then pour out a libation of beer, buttermilk, and date honey. Perform the washing of the mouth and then say three times the incantation . . . and then remove the offerings. Take the hand of the god and then seat him in the garden under the *urigallu* (this Sumerian word has not the same meaning as in the New Year ritual where it means 'high priest'; here it means 'reed hut,' or 'standard') on the reed mat, in a linen covering. Turn his face to the west. Go to the river and then throw pease meal into the river. Pour out a *mihhu* libation. Raise your hand and repeat the incantations 'Father of the Abyss' and 'Brink of the Abyss' . . . three times each before the river, and then set water in the seven pots of holy water, and then place them in the (shrine) of KU.BU. In the pots of holy water everything for the washing of the mouth, a tamarisk, a . . . plant, . . . seven slips of cedars, a cloth made of reeds, a marsh reed, good reeds, . . . sulphur . . . salt, (gum of) a cedar, a cypress and turpentine . . . EL-plant, wool, oil, the stones *šabanu sabitu . . . mušgarru, samtu,* lapis lazuli, UD.AS, UDAS.AS, *dušu* . . . Ninurta-stone, oil of the best quality, *nigulu*-oil, cedar oil, date honey, butter you should throw . . . of the offerings their essences you should put, and then set forth. *Bukinnu*-wood, tamarisk, water of the pots for holy water, . . . *bukinnu*-wood, the stone *samtu*, lapis lazuli, silver quartz, gold quartz, turpentine, oil of millet you should put thereon and then . . . pots of holy water on the brick of the Lady of the Gods (Beltis) you should set . . . pots of holy water you should prepare and then perform the washing of the mouth. Then you should remove the offering. (Nine offerings) for Anu, Enlil, Ea, Sin, Shamash, Adad, Marduk, Gula, Ishtar, the stars (the Igigi) you should prepare. Repeat the incantation 'Tamarisk, holy tree' and then perform the washing of the mouth. (Nine) offerings for NIN. MAH, KU.BU, NIN.A.HA.KUD.DU, NIN.KUR.RA, NIN. A.GAL, GUSKIN.BAN.DA, NIN.ILDU, NIN.ZA.DIM and that god (facing) northwards you should prepare. As before. Two offerings for SAG.ME.GAR and Dilbat you should prepare. As before. Two offerings for Sin and Lulim you should prepare. As before. Three offerings for the Bull, the *mešri*-star and Nibeanu you should prepare. As before. Six offerings for the Scales, the House of Shamash, the Plough, the star SU.PA, the Chariot, the star *Eru*, the Goat you should prepare. As before. Four offerings for the Field, the Swallow, Anunitum, the Ear of Corn you should prepare. As before. Three offerings for the stars of the Anu-way, the Enlil-way, and the Ea-way you should prepare. As before. In the morning inside the canopy you should put chairs for Ea, Shamash, and Marduk. Lay out the *hussitu* garments. Draw a linen cloth thereon. Prepare three dishes. Present dates, A.TIR meal. Place a conserve of date honey and butter. Set forth a pot *adagurru*. Six (or seven) pots. . . . Continue to throw . . . plant therein. Find 'the fruit of the garden,' pluck it, and then lay out. . . . Offer sifted barley-(meal). Offer a censer of turpentine. . . . Raise your hand and then repeat three times the incantation 'Thou who art born in heaven from its wind.' The incantation '. . . ,' the incantation 'Juice of the twig for that god (whether) whole (or) halved' you should repeat, and then offer. . . . Throw pease-meal on the forehead of the ram and then sacrifice it. Prepare the offerings. The deacon (*mashmashu*-priest) should stand on the left of that god. Repeat before Ea, Shamash, and Marduk the incantation 'Exalted. . . .' Repeat three times the incantation 'Ea, Shamash, and Marduk.' Repeat the incantation 'Shamash . . .' and then perform the washing of the mouth. Thereafter repeat the incantation 'Holy image that art perfected by a great ritual,' and then smear the side of the. . . . A whispered prayer you should whisper, you should remove yourself . . . and then all those craftsmen who have been in contact with the god, and the gear . . . (of) the KU.BU, NIN.A.GAL, GUSKIN.BAN.DA, NIN. ILDU, NIN.ZA.DIM, you should set, and then a cord on . . . you should bind. Cut the tamarisk with a dagger . . . you should say, 'Open the eyes of that god. The deacon should stand before that god. . . .' Repeat the incantation 'In they going forth, in thy going forth,' with (each) pace. The incantation 'Image that art born from the holy,' the incantation 'Image that art born in heaven,' the incantation 'NIN.ILDU, mighty carpenter of heaven' . . . and then . . . the incantation 'Exalted tiara,' the incantation 'Bright throne' you should repeat and before . . . repeat the incantation 'In heaven thou shalt not stand.' Repeat again and then repeat three times 'Thou shalt enter the . . .' and then. . . . In the first place remove the offering for that god.

Thereafter remove that of KU.BU and NIN.A.HA.KUD.DU. Thereafter the craftsmen should remove (the offerings of). . . . Thereafter remove the offerings of the great gods. Take the hand of the god and then the incantation 'Foot that advanceth, foot that advanceth . . . ,' the incantation 'In his going in the street' you should repeat (as you come) up to the temple of the god. In the gate of the temple of the god you should have regard to the *muhhuru* offerings. Take the hand of the god and lead him in and then repeat the incantation 'My king in thy goodness of heart' (till you come) up to the shrine. Set the god on his seat, and then repeat at his (seat) the incantation 'Place that is the *qisikku* of heaven' (and) the incantation 'Ornament of the exalted chapel.' At the side of the shrine put up a canopy. Prepare an offering for Ea and Marduk. Complete the offering and then perform the washing of the mouth. Purify that god with juice of the *bukinnu* and then repeat the incantation 'Asar (Marduk), Good Being, son of Eridu' seven times, and then bring up everything of the divinity. Put (it) on by night. Place (him) at the edge of the abyss, and then make his bright garment, twice treated by the fuller, reach the edge of the abyss.

"Let initiate instruct initiate, he shall not let the uninitiated see; it is a thing forbidden of Enlil, the elder, (and) Marduk (or, of the great lord, Marduk). According to the wording of the tablet (which is) a copy, in agreement with the interpretation of Nabu-etil-ilani the son of Dabibi, the incantation priest, Iddina-Nabu, the son of Gahul-Tutu, the deacon, wrote to preserve his life, to lengthen his days, and (placed in Esagila)."

(7) *Rituals Relating* to *the* Lilissu-drum

The sacred drum, known as the *lilissu*, played an important part on many religious occasions, and certain rituals were carried out at the making or repairing of the *lilissu*. The ceremony of mouth-washing, given in the previous text, was performed for the *lilissu*, showing that the sacred drum was regarded and treated as a god. The text of these rituals has been published by the late F. Thureau-Dangin in *Rituels Accadiens*, 1921.

AO. 6479

"When you are about (to cover) the bronze *lilissu*, a black bull, perfect, sound in horns and hoofs, should be examined from head to tail by an experienced temple servant. If the body of the bull is as black as pitch, it may be taken for the rites and observances. But if it is spotted with seven white hairs like a star, or if it has been struck with a rod, or touched with a whip, it should not be taken for the rites and observances.

"When you have to have the bull brought into the workshop, on a favorable day you should stand beside the bull, you should (sweep?) the floor, sprinkle holy water . . . the workshop. You should place two bricks on the right side and on the left of the gate of the workshop. You should pour out a libation to the gods of heaven, to the gods of heaven and earth and the great gods. You should offer the best beer. You should have the bull brought into the workshop. You should place a reed mat; you should pour sand under the mat and surround the sides of the mat with it. You should place that bull on the reed mat and tie it by the (leg?) with a goat's-hair cord. You should place beer from the *sapu*-plant in a bronze drum (*uppu*) before the bull.

"You should set out two holy-water pots for KU.SUR and NIN.A.HA.KUD.DU. You should set out two reed offering tables. You should place seven loaves of wheat and seven loaves of spelt apiece for them. You should set out milk, beer, and date wine. You should set out an *adagurru*-pot . . . cypress . . . a drinking pot you should set out . . . one-third of a mina of white wool . . . seven and a half minas of goat's hair you should place. Beer from the *sapu*-plant . . . a pole of boxwood . . . thorn . . . you should put a holy-water pot, oil of cedarwood, honey, fine fat . . . you should set; (you should purify) with censers and torch . . . the thigh and the *hinsu*-flesh; you should present roast meats; you should pour out the best beer, wine, and milk . . . you should place . . . the holy-water pot . . . you should place twelve bricks.

"You should put twelve linen cloths before them, and upon them you should seat the twelve gods. You should draw water from the holy-water pot of NIN.A.HA.KUD.DU, and should sanctify the prepared offerings; twelve tables of offerings you should set out; you should sacrifice twelve lamb offerings; the thigh, the *hinsu*-flesh, and the roast meats you should present; beer, wine, and milk you should offer; you should pour out seed-grain. You should set up the *lilissu*.

"You should place one brick for LUM.HA. You should set up one table of offerings and sacrifice one lamb-sacrifice; you should present the thigh, the *hinsu*-flesh, and the roast meats; you should offer the best beer, wine, and milk; you should set water before the gods. You should stretch out the hangings. For that bull you should perform the rite of the washing of the mouth. With a pipe of sweet-smelling reed you should whisper the incantation 'Great bull, exalted bull, treading the holy herbage,' into his right ear, and in the same way, into his left ear, the incantation: 'O bull, spawn of Zu!' You should sprinkle him with essence of cedar and purify him with censer and torch; with *zisurru* (flour paste) you should surround him. You should take up your stand by the head of the bull and recite NI.TUG. KI NIGIN.NA to the sound of the bronze drum. After that, recite DIM.ME.IR etc. Then you should fell that bull, and burn its heart with cedar, cypress, and pease-meal in a fire of cedar-wood before the *lilissu*. You should take out the tendon of the left shoulder. You should bury the carcass of that bull in a red cloth and cast oil of *gunnu* upon it. You should place it facing the west. You should take the skin of that bull and you should steep it in fine flour of holy corn in water, the best beer, and wine. You should put it in fine fat of a clean bull with spices from the heart of their plants, four *qa* of flour of millet, four *qa* of *bitqa* flour, and one *qa* of *kurru* flour. You should press it with walnut and alum from the land of the Hittites. With the skin thus prepared you should cover the bronze *lilissu*.

"You should stretch one linen cord thereon. You should overlay with holy varnish the drumsticks of *musukannu* wood, boxwood, cedar, *usu*, and all the rest of the drumsticks of hard wood for the bronze *lilissu*. With the tendon of the left shoulder you should close the opening of the drum and unloose the linen cord. You should place a *napdu* upon (the drum). You should bury the contents of the stomach. You should then make ready prepared sacrifices for LUM.HA and sacrifice a lamb-offering, present the thigh, the *hinsu*-flesh, and the roast meats, and offer the best beer, wine, and milk. (Then follows a list of the twelve gods mentioned above:)

> Anu, Enlil, and Ea, the great gods;
> Lugal-gir-ra and Mes-lam-ta-e-a;
> Nin-sig who dwells in Nippur;
> Su-zi-an-na of the Abyss;
> En-nu-gi who tills the fields;
> Ku-sur, the high lord;
> Nin-sar, child of E-sab-ba;
> Nin-ka-si, child of the new city;
> Nusku, child of the thirtieth day, the day of the *bubbulu*
>   (i.e., the disappearance of the moon).

On the fifteenth day you should bring out the bronze *lilissu* before Shamash. You should prepare the things necessary for five sacrifices for Ea, Shamash, Marduk, Lum-ha, and *Lilissu*. You should offer a lamb-sacrifice and present the thigh, *hinsu*-flesh, and roast meats, with offerings of best beer, wine, and milk. You should perform the rites of purification with censer and torch and the cleansing of holy water.

"You should then recite EN.KI UTU etc., three times. You should perform the rite of the washing of the mouth (for the *lilissu*.) With fine fat and *halsu*-oil you should anoint it. The chief *kalû* should lay . . . upon the *lilissu.* The things necessary for the sacrifices you should now remove. You should purify the *lilissu* with censer and torch; you should take the hand of the *lilissu* and bring it before the gods; you should place it among the seed-grain; lastly you should make the lamentation LUGAL.E etc.

"The young priest may see these rites which you perform, but the stranger who does not possess the hereditary knowledge of the rites shall not see them, unless he wishes his days to be shortened. The initiated shall reveal them to the initiated; the uninitiated shall not see them. It is among the forbidden things of Anu, Enlil, and Ea, the great gods."

BIBLIOGRAPHY

Behrens, E. *Assyrische-Babylonische Briefe kultischen Inhalts.* Leipzig, 1906.

Dhorme, E. *Les Religions de Babylonie et d'Assyrie.* Paris, 1945.

Driver, G. R., and Sir J. C. Miles. *The Assyrian Laws.* Oxford, 1935.

Ebeling, E. *Aus dem Tagewerk eines assyrischen Zauberpriesters.* Leipzig, 1931.

———. *Tod und Leben nach den Vorstellungen der Babylonier.* Leipzig, 1931.

Engnell, Ivan. *Studies in Divine Kingship in the Ancient Near East.* Uppsala, 1945.

Fossey, C. *La Magie Assyrienne.* Paris, 1902.

Frankfort, H. *Cylinder Seals.* London, 1939.

———, ed. *The Intellectual Adventure of Ancient Man.* Chicago, 1946.

———. *Kingship and the Gods.* Chicago, 1948.

Gadd, C. J. *Ideas of Divine Rule in the Ancient East.* London, 1948. (Schweich Lectures, 1945.)

Harper, R. F. *The Code of Hammurabi.* Chicago, 1904.

Hooke, S. H., ed. *Myth and Ritual.* Oxford, 1933.

———, ed. *Myth, Ritual, and Kingship.* Oxford, 1958.

———. *The Origins of Early Semitic Ritual.* London, 1938. (Schweich Lectures, 1935.)

Jastrow, M. *Babylonian-Assyrian Birth-Omens.* Giessen, 1914.

———. *Die Religion Babyloniens und Assyriens.* Giessen, 1912.

Jirku, A. *Das weltliche Recht im Alten Testament.* Gütersloh, 1927.

King, L. W. *Babylonian Magic and Sorcery.* London, 1896.

———. *Chronicles Concerning Early Babylonian Kings.* London, 1907.

———. *A History of Babylon.* London, 1915.

——. *A History of Sumer and Akkad.* London, 1910.

——. *Legends of Babylon and Egypt.* London, 1918. (Schweich Lectures, 1916.)

Kramer, S. N. *Sumerian Mythology.* Philadelphia, 1944.

Kraus, F. R. *Die physiognomischen Omina der Babylonier.* Leipzig, 1935.

Langdon, S. *Babylonian Menologies and the Semitic Calendars.* London, 1935. (Schweich Lectures, 1933.)

——. *The Legend of Etana and the Eagle.* Paris, 1932.

Meier, G. *Die assyrische Beschwörungssammlung Maqlu.* Berlin, 1937.

Meissner, B. *Babylonien und Assyrien.* 2 vols. Heidelberg, 1925.

Müller, K. F. *Das assyrische Ritual.* Leipzig, 1937.

Pallis, S. A. *The Babylonian Akitu Festival.* Copenhagen, 1926.

Pfeiffer, R. H. *State Letters of Assyria.* New Haven, 1935.

Pritchard, J. B., ed. *Ancient Near Eastern Texts Relating to the Old Testament.* Princeton, 1950.

Smith, Sidney. *The Early History of Assyria.* London, 1928.

Tallqvist, K. *Akkadische Götterepitheta.* Leipzig, 1938.

Thompson, R. Campbell, trans. *The Devils and Evil Spirits of Babylonia.* London, 1903–1904.

——. *Semitic Magic.* London, 1908.

Thureau-Dangin, F. *Rituels Accadiens.* Paris, 1921.

INDEX

Index

Ecclesiastes: 101
Eclipses: 93ff.
Elam: 80, 86, 92
Enkidu: 64f., 68, 83, 99f.
Enlil, storm-god: 13, 16f., 19, 24, 27, 62, 66, 74, 91, 93
Entu: 27
Erech: 22, 67
Ereshkigal, underworld goddess: 23f., 38, 46, 71
Eridu: 18, 107
Esagila: 43, 54, 63, 104, 106ff.
Esarhaddon: 43, 86, 90
Etana, myth of: 4, 70
Etemenanki, ziqqurat of Babylon: 44, 112

Figurines, protective: 26
Flood: xi, 4, 18, 21 f., 60, 63f., 66ff.
Foundation deposits: 9
Frankfort, H.: v, 9f., 27ff., 63, 70

Gadd, C. J.: 63, 68, 93
Gilgamesh: xi, xiv, 4, 8–9, 22, 60, 63ff., 83, 99–100
Gira, fire-god: 116–17
Gudea, King of Lagash: 15, 21, 43–44, 74, 83f.
Gula, goddess: 119; temple of, 42

Hammurabi: 4, 9, 12, 20, 31, 47, 75, 97
Herodotus: 3
Hittite, pictographic script: xii
Horus: 27

Igigi, gods of heaven: 25, 103, 105, 119
Immortality: 67, 99
Indus civilization: xii
Irra, plague-god: 24
Ishtar, goddess: 16, 19, 21 ff., 24–25, 26, 30f., 34f., 47, 65, 66f., 71, 90f., 93, 98, 113, 119

Jacobsen, T.: 13, 59, 61, 63, 79f.
Job, the Babylonian: 98–99
Jupiter: 95

Kalu-priests: 45–46, 104, 107, 125
Kingship: 7f., 27f., 49, 64, 70, 97
Kingu: 25, 61 f., 115

Index

Sargon I: 87
Saturn: 95
Sennacherib: 84
Shamash: 11 f., 19ff., 41, 77, 82, 112f., 119
Shurpu: 5, 74, 98
Sin, god of Sippar: 11, 19f., 25, 27, 41, 68, 90f., 93, 112f., 119
Sin, confession of: 98f.
Sirius: 22
Smith, George: xi
Smith, Sidney: v, xiii, 31 n., 118
Smith, W. R.: xiii
Speiser, E. A.: 63
Subartu: 92
Substitution, ritual of: 36–39, 46, 51 f., 77
Sumerian civilization: xi ff., 7ff.

Tablets of Destiny: 17, 61 f., 70
Tammuz, Sumerian god: 22, 29ff., 37, 46, 52, 69, 71, 80
Tashmetu: 43
Tell el-Amarna, tablets of: 69
Teshub: *see* Adad
Thureau-Dangin, F.: 39, 122
Tiamat, Chaos-dragon: 13, 15, 25, 53, 60ff., 91
Tower of Babel: 43f.

Urash: 28
Urigallu, chief priest: 45, 103ff.
Urshanabi: 66
Urukagina: 48f., 82, 97
Utnapishtim: 65ff.
Utukku: 16, 25, 35

Venus: *see* Dilbat

Weather, divination by: 89, 95f.

Yahweh: 21, 34f., 52, 89, 101

Zarpanit: 43, 104ff., 112, 115f.
Ziqqurat: 43f., 53, 73, 92
Zu, storm-bird: 17, 70, 114f., 123

BABYLONIAN AND ASSYRIAN RELIGION

has been set in ten-point Janson, a face designed in seventeenth-century Europe and regarded today as one of our most legible book faces. The initial display letter chosen for this book is Sistina, a contemporary European type design which combines pleasingly with the Janson letter form.

University of Oklahoma Press

Norman